Truth
A prayer to a full moon for Truth…

Graham McCumber

ISBN: 1986211274
ISBN-13: 9781986211277

DEDICATION

I dedicate this book to my mom and to people who suffer and are not recognized nor helped. My mother, who has by now earned much respect in the science world continues to operate on the faith that everything will work out, and it does. You mentored me during some pretty dark/hard times and now times are getting brighter. No more tears (only healthy ones from your son.) Pain is a dualistic phenomenon that is necessary in this binary life so that we can feel it's contrast, which feels rewarding. To be clutched in prolonged pain, with no peer support or even recognition is an element of defeat in its own. I was so fortunate to have my mom and others who supported me when I was in need of it, like my aunts and uncles. I have met people who had bad cases of ratlung and were in a strong suffering state with very limited support-this book I dedicate to them.

And..

To Dr. Jasmine, from Vietnam. Thank you for prescribing me the winning pharmaceutical medicine, "Amitriptyline." With intuitive reasoning you were able to find the chemical balancing medicine that would get me a good night sleep. For that, you are my angelic savior! You changed my world that was getting so grim and negative. Now, I can count on a good night sleep; something that I haven't been able to do since before ratlung. So, now I can carry on with my life. Dedications to you too. Kam on bang, Dr. Jasmine-

Mark smith, a Dr. at Hilo medical center. Mark, you believed in me when not every other doctor did. You came in and checked on me even though I wasn't even your patient. You had me flewen to Queens hospital in Oahu for better medical help, which saved my life. This book I dedicate to you too also.

To Dr. William pettis, my acupuncturist. Another one of those people who never gave up on me. Will you treated me for free or work trade (gardening or cleaning.) Your work moved locations several times, but I always rode my bike to your place of business to reciene needles and Chinese medicine treatments. You were inspiration for me as you have transcended many states of poor health as yourself. A dedication also goes out to you Will.

Stacy, my speech therapist from the Hilo hospital. You believed in me too when there were few who did and for that I also dedicate my book to you. You fed me ice cubes just after the coma when I wanted to eat something but frozen water was all that I was permitted to eat. I dedicate a piece of my book to you Stacy.

To all of the nurses at Hilo hospital: The nurses are hospitals real care providers. Sweet in their nature, selfless in their ways, taking care of sick and injured people because they feel compassion for helping. Ellie, my Phillipeno nurse who I thought was my girlfriend when I was comatosed (because she bathed me and dressed me ext.) You told me stories of the Philippines and your growing up life in Philippines, which would make me smile. Thank you and dedications to you too.

CONTENTS

ACKNOWLEDGMENTS

Here's acknowledge all the people in my book:

Arthur Dodge: You helped me with my gofundme for Hebat and multiple other projects. In fact, Arthur you are the person who said, "you should write your book now" and so shortly after I started it! Thank you, Arthur!

Caterina Dodge: Arthur's beautiful wife. She once saved me from drowning in the warm ponds very shortly after the coma in water just too deep to stand in. Cat and Arthur are both my longest standing friends from Hawaii. I knew them from before my illness back when I first moved to Hawaii. Thanks guys for being great friends!

Lyn Howe: my aunt in Wahwah-she is the medicine woman who first diagnosed me with ratlung. I lived at her and Geoff's house multiple times in Hawaii; she has instilled me with wisdom in numerous deep talks we so often shared.

Geoff Rauch my uncle, Lyn's husband. An organic farmer. I got much of my organic farming knowledge from both Geoff and Lyn. Thank Lyn and Geoff!

Kay Howe: my mom-she moved into the hospital, and we have lived together ever since. She sustained my life when I was so fragile because of my injury, and mom it was because of you alone that I was able to reach the place where I am today. You raised me twice and are allowing me a chance to regain independence. Thank you, mom!

Neil McCumber: my awesome older brother-came to the hospital while I was in a coma, was present when I decided to live when I was expected to die. Thanks, Niel!

Caydie McCumber: my beloved sister-found blue water lily when thoughts were grim of finding it. She has been very supportive to me (as much as can). Thanks, Caydie!

Harrison: A good friend from post ratlung-has done countless favors for me including cutting down the weed trees that loomed over my garden, robbing precious light. Also gave me employment when times were hard. He gave me medicine. Thank you, love you, big buddy!

David Hubbard: Hilo's revered oil paint artist-was in front of a canvas always painting another real life/abstract, while surrounded by his girls (pot plants.) Thanks, David!

Kavika-heavy set neighbor from 331 B East Lanikaula, sold me weed. Thanks, Kavika. The best of wishes to you and your family!

Greg and Patty Howe My wonderful aunt and uncle who lived in Freeport Bahamas. I stayed with them and free dove for an entire summer. I also went and visited them with my mom post ratlung. Thanks guys for being a big part of my life!

Kay -neighbor-sold me weed.

Rudi-neighbor-sold me weed.

Jacob Medina-Hilo famous Artist/friend

Martin therapist from Kapoho taught me about ight or flight jacking up the nervous system.

More acknowledgments:

Dr. Alan Thal Dr. from Hawi who recommended me to take buffered vitamin C to alleviate my constipation.

Sheri Thal Dr. Alan Thal's daughter and my voice/music teacher.

Fred Smith owner of Smith point, where I stayed each time in the Bahamas.

Amy Slay Sylvia's older sister and Fred's girlfriend and my cousin. Wearing a bikini at Pohohiki's boat launch, she and Julie Jay Rock distracted the drivers of a fishing boat with their striking women parts, and they almost ran me over.

Tom Handcock aka Tommy Thai boxer is the divvy from Ferry Hill England who dove with sharks and balanced them for tourists. Tom and Sylvia are now married with two children.

Julie Jay-rock Amy's friend with the big boobs at Pohohiki's boat launch.

Susan Salas-My colon hydro therapist.

Jen Rasperson, my friend from Wah, wah-gets me Sativa.

Christian Coyal My first and most dynamic yoga teacher.

Mary Chapman-handstand Mary/my banyon tree climbing trainer.

Racheal yoga teacher.

Sarah Yoga teacher.

Crystal Yaminmoto neighbor friend in Hilo who helped me move my table for keiki (baby) plants in my garden.

Albert Talarock, My young blood friend who played "Spirit ball" with Hebat and I.

Bob Kirk Boss and he also built the house with us. Had surreal hallucination of blue baby Krishnya with him in a hospital visit.

Asherd #1 co-worker together we were building a house in Kehena Hawaii 2007.

Adrien Ferril #2 co-worker together were building a house in Kehena Hawaii 2007.

Donald Trump Fucking asshole leader possessed by his ego.

Adolf Hitler Fucking asshole leader possessed by his ego.

Nhako bear and Medicine for the people An awesome band (Med for the peep's) genius songwriter/performer (Nhako.) I have the same hair cut as Nhako bear.

Dek Gin Rudi's Balinese son from my trip with mom to Indo.

Dave Hotchner moms friend who we care-took his house in Java's Tembei.

Fred Smith Amy's gracious boyfriend who let us stay in his colorful beach house.

Jerry Slay my cousin and work/skate/surf/weed growing partner. We moved to Hawaii together in 2006. RIP amigo.

Sylvia Slay Amy and Jerry's lil sister. She found Yoda (Greg and Patty's dog) when she was a bald Pot cake on the street.

Tom Handcock, The English bloke, married to Slyvia, Sylvia's husband

Julie J Rock Amy's friend with big boobs that together with Amy's great ass distracted two fisher men almost to run me over, but my guardian angel saved me.

Greg Howe, My free diver uncle from the Bahamas.

Patty Howe My free diver aunt also in (was in) the Bahamas.

Baziznitch family Jamie B, Marian B, Ray B, Amy B family from my childhood town of Goodland Florida. They recently invited me on a week vacation to Molokai HI, where I had a pivotal time in my ratlung recovery

Varushka and Aaron friends (couple) I attended hand stand workshop with them, taught by the dynamo handstand Mary Chapm

Bub Prat Owner of Ku'ku'au studio. He and Sheri held recitals at the Ku'ku'au.

Pak Mangku, a Balinese metaphysical healer who worked on me while I was deep in the coma.

Madison McShaw a divine feminine light being and an indigo child here on this earth to spread light in this time where it is so desperately needed.

Truth

"A prayer to a full moon for Truth..."

A journey through hardship for Truth.

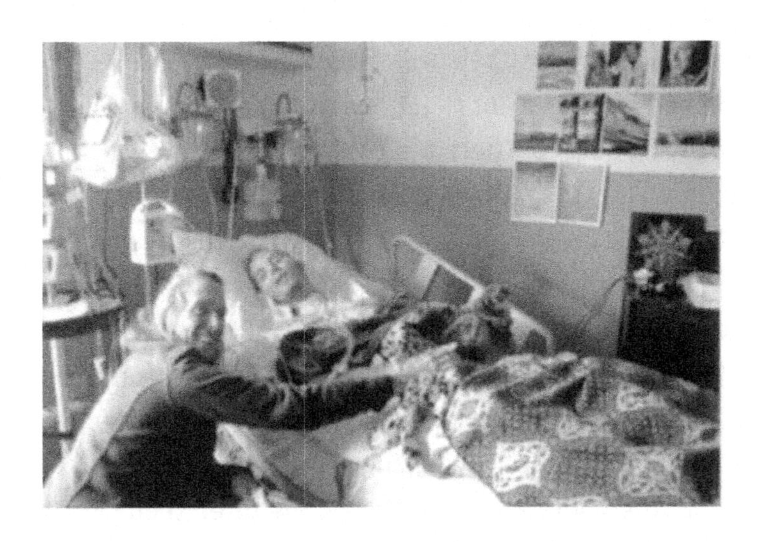

1
Life before Rat lungworm

Before I got ratlung, I was a surfer, skateboarding, working fool. I was really getting my life going. I lived in Kapoho Hawaii, just a short commute to the waves in my truck. I surfed daily, or I would feel off if I missed a day. I also skateboarded regularly at the skate park in Pahoa, which was a thirty-minute commute from where we stayed. I worked in the construction trade, building houses with Bob Kirk, who was the boss. Aside from Bob, there were also Adrien and Asher whom I worked with. Asher was the more experienced of the two, putting Adrien behind him on skill rank, but I liked them both and looked up to them, especially Asher. I also privately built rock walls and patios with my cousin Jerry Slay, whom I lived and worked with. We also were both hired by Bob to help build the house. We did some foundation stone work, making big berm rock walls, which were used for growing decorative plants for the bridge to rest on, which was connected to the front door entrance.

Jerry was also the first person who I successfully grew weed with. He had a sativa plant that grew as tall as the banana trees it was growing next to. There are two varieties of weed, Sativa, and Indica. Of course, there is a high bred too, which is a cross of the two. Indica is the most widely grown of the two IN Hawaii, so Sativa is harder to come by, which is a "make you want to do project high," as opposed to a "body high," which Indica is. Sometimes, I would get Sativa from my friend Jen, cause that is all she smokes. She likes the up high as opposed to the "I feel like I wanna take a nap high." I took to sticking my plants in the lava field, where I put them into a puka (hole.) Of the three seed's I got from my friend Will Jill, one was mango kush. It smelled just like a mango, "a marijuana mango plant!" My girls were all Indica's! In the lava field, weed plants get great sunlight, but you must be careful of rippers (people who steel plants), and choppers (helicopters.) Jerry was also my surfing/skating work buddy. We moved to Hawaii together but eventually, we spent too much time in close quarters, so we parted ways. Then I got sick and went into the coma some months after that. After moving back to New Mexico from Hawaii, Jerry got a parole that disallowed his weed smoking habit. Then, at twenty-seven he died for reasons of the regulations disallowing him to smoke weed, or else he would be incarcerated. His choice to smoke "spice," which is a synthetic herb substitute that you can buy on the internet led to him having a heart attack. A side effect is that it makes your heart speed up real fast; that's what my uncle said when he tried some when offered by Jerry. Later in the hospital, Jerry had a heart attack and died at twenty-eight. We had spent some time hanging out after the coma before he went back to the mainland for his unexpected early departure.

Jerry and I bringing ply-wood for making mini pipe (half pipe.)

2

What Rat lungworm disease is

Angiostrongylus cantonensis the rat lungworm is a parasitic nematode that causes rat lungworm disease. Infection in humans is called angiostrongyliasis or rat lungworm disease and is the leading cause of eosinophilic meningitis worldwide. The parasite was first identified in Hawaii in the 1950's, with the first human cases of RLWD occurring in 1959-1960. The parasite is now found in approximately 30 countries including the southeast Gulf Coast states of the U.S. The nematode uses various species of rats as definitive hosts, and a wide range of slug and snail species as intermediate hosts.

Male and female adult rat lungworms reproduce in the pulmonary artery of the rat. Eggs are flushed to the rat's lungs where they embryonate and hatch. Hatched larvae migrate up the rat's bronchial tree, are swallowed, and excreted in feces. Slugs and snails consume infected rat feces and harbor the 1st through 2nd stage larvae. It is the 3rd stage larvae that are infective to humans and other animals, including their rat host. Rats eat slugs and snails and become infected. The parasite survives the gut acid, burrows through the intestinal wall, and navigates its way to the rat's brain and central nervous system via the bloodstream. There the larvae molt from 3rd stage larvae to 4th and then 5th stage or young adults. When ready to reproduce, the larvae leave the rat's brain and travel through the heart to the pulmonary artery and lungs, where they breed and begin the cycle again.

The disease is often associated with the accidental consumption of a terrestrial slug or snail on fresh, uncooked produce; however, it also may potentially be transmitted through rainwater catchment. The arrival of the semi-slug *Parmarion martensi* on Hawai'i Island near the turn of the millennium corresponds with the increase and severity of human cases of *A. cantonensis* infection. This slug is an effective host with an infection rate of near 78%. The disease has caused mortality and morbidity in Hawai‘i, with the most significant percentage of cases occurring on Hawai`i Island

3
Bali

I am a traveling man at heart. I started when I was seventeen and a half when I embarked on my first journey across seas to Bali Indonesia, where I have an aunt and uncle who live. I lived with and amongst the Balinese people in the inland-artisan village of Ubud, studying Indonesian and learning about the culture. I was recognized as the albino Balinese in that village, just so you get a sense of how connected to the people I was. In Bali, there are many deep-rooted beliefs that the Balinese people abide by that don't make sense to the heavily conditioned Westerners mind. That is because they each have a different belief of "reality." In Bali, it is the custom, or tradition to use your right hand for eating and shaking hands (greeting,) whereas the left one is used for wiping your butt and more kasar (rude) things. I adapted their beliefs for the entire six months I stayed there. They let me carry a decorated piece of bamboo in a procession that a large group of Balinese men carried called a Galongon. They accepted me as one of them, and with them, I went to Temple ceremonies throughout Bali with the family. I dressed in a surang (traditional prayer dress) and prayed at temple ceremonies. I was in no way a tourist for that trip. I ate at all the local warungs (*restaurants*), shopped at the pasar (*markets*), and did everything in the manner of a Balinese, like eating with my right hand, and wiping my butt with my left hand. I made a girlfriend who was a cewek desa (*village girl*), so all the more reasons to learn Bahasa. Her name is Vita (Pita) and she's a jegeg (hottie), and a real sweetheart to boot. I practiced night and day, always learning new words and practiced using them in speech on her and the locals. I got several opportunities to take surf trips to various surf locations on the island, where I would rent the hotel paling murah (*the cheapest hotel)* and surf on pristine waves (umbak bagus.) Indo's waves are perfect, although the waves in Kuta beach can have large swarms of garbage, as Bali is very plastic polluted. My surf trips were much different than the cultural experiences I got when living in Ubud. I opted to riding the local bimo bus instead of the tour bus when I would return to Ubud, had I ventured to the pantai (beach) to go surf for a few days.

I met many healers in Bali and had the privilege of learning from them. A Javinese healer, Roni, who was a foot reflexologist with a whole understanding of the workings of energy, is one healer I once worked with. A healer may do things that seem peculiar or strange, but they are merely being connected with their own True animal self. This is how they can offer healing; it is not the healer who is doing the healing, but rather tis thee being the conduit to be a channel to God. The healer is merely a human being with enough compassion to recognize the suffering of others and want to provide help. Anybody has the "healer potential," you just need to be receptive of it, and humility brings receptivity. A healer is conscious of his/her own human potential. Healers are notorious for burping as a means of clearing stuck-stale energy when they are active in healing. Pak Bayu would raise and lower his hair, while Pak Mangku scribbles in Sanskrit with his hand on the *lantai* tile floor. I did not bother to ask of his reason for doing this, but I assumed he was transcribing a message to the Gods. It was in Bali where I developed the desire to be a healer myself one day. I recognized then that anybody has the ability to be a healer, so I too have the ability. I was fascinated! First, I would have to endure much more pain and hardship before I could have the compassion it takes to be a healer. Pain and hardships, like sickness, can bring out the ego. It can also bring awakening once you endure more pain and grief than you think is humanly possible. That's when encounters with divinity and ego are most frequent too. If you fall unconscious and so your ego takes you over don't get discouraged. "It's not your fault, just go back to being present. Just be present and ask for guidance from the divine mother. To be a healer, you must be able to see the Truth and be able to detect fraud or over-exaggerated ego as well. This goes the same for recognizing your own ego. "Only when we can recognize the ego in ourselves is when our true nature will come out, and when we are present with our True selves, in this time of world crisis can we be of help. Ego simply is a human condition, so with will and choice, "choose not to listen."

4
India

My plane landed at 4:30 in the morning in New Delhi India. I was just nineteen years old with my big orange backpack that my uncle Peter had gifted me before I left. I remember boarding the Bart subway late at night in Berkeley to go to the SFO, where I had an overnight flight to India. I had a layover where I was put up for the night and fed two meals in Taipei, Taiwan. My brothers and sister seemed to think I was crazy for going to India alone. I did not have any friends who were close enough or had interest in traveling around India though. This was a soul journey anyways! If you travel with friends from home then you are not obligated to make new friends in order for social connection, which allows for personal growth and you may/will fall into old conditioned patterns. For this reason, you will not grow new neural pathways, broadening your perception, essentially pushing evolutional growth by you allowing yourself to not think of them as strange tribes people or dirty savages, but rather a part of the fellow human being family and absorb their ways with an open curious heart, accepting their approach to life as a legitimate way to live. So much enjoyment can be had by connecting with peoples of a different region, with a different culture.

When I landed early that morning, I caught a ride with an Indian couple returning to India after visiting the Bay area. They brought me to a dirty little strip of hotels about forty minutes from the airport. I walked into a hotel and somebody sleeping behind the counter somewhere quickly woke up and came to check me in. "Do you have any water" I asked. He says while bobbing his head, "pani nahi, which means no water." Then he held up a bottle of Fanta. I don't really drink soda under these circumstances, "it was 2 AM and I was soon to go to bed!" Plus, too much refined sugar is bad for me. I kindly declined the Fanta and he brought me to my room. Huge mosquitoes loomed in the room ready to drink whoever's blood is in the area. The paranoia of malaria weighed heavy on my chest as I laid in the bed trying to turn my mind off for a bit before morning. When daylight hit the hustle-bustle began. At first light, townspeople started to stir as India's City woke up. Indian men cooked big pots of "Chai tea." They ladled it into cups, which they sold for a Rupi, and they called out "chai" as they sold it. I made sure I grabbed all my stuff, then I checked out. The mission of my first day was to board a bus going to Old Delhi, as it had many olden style buildings and it sounded more enchanting of a place to experience than New Delhi, which had a lot of the industries and corporate India world. In India, so dirty is the ground and flies are all around. A bus pulled up and I got in and sat down. I quickly checked through my travel belt to make sure I had everything. "Wait stop the bus; I forgot my passport!" The crowded bus just trekked on while all the Indian faces looked at me wondering what my problem was. I looked through my money belt again and found my passport. Relief filled me. "Never mind, found it" I said. I did not want to lose my passport at the start of the trip! I checked into a hotel in old Delhi where I felt out the town for a few days. Everything was so interesting, and there were strange foods like deep fried orange sugar paste swirly pastries and the most uniquely spiced dahl with chapatti. Chapati is a Indian style flat bread, "like a Tortilla!" The spices used in India have uniquely distinct flavor, and the odors were just as uncommon to me. Curd or yogurt lassis were often sought out by me for their probiotic properties which fed my good gut flora. Mango lassies are also bomb-diggity too!

When I had enough of the crowded city experience, which was quite quickly, I craved for nature of the Himalayas. While in Delhi in a travel counsel agency with many different agents, I remember there being Indian people everywhere and in the crowd, an adult Indian man quickly approached me with a pamphlet of pictures of his houseboat, inside and out. He said "hello, I am Abdul, what is your good name? You must get out of Delhi, too hot and polluted here!" Naive nineteen-year-old me, was jostled into going to stay on his house-boat in Dahl lake in Kashmire. He wanted me to pay extra money and fly there on his private plane. I said "no, I want to take the bus and experience India, I'm taking the all-day, all-night bus ride!" I arrived at Dhal lake in Kashmir, where his houseboat was located, and I found my way to the dock, which was on the edge of the lake. The town was polluted with Indian soldiers, who were currently then fighting a war with Pakistan. I looked out in the center of the lake and saw the houseboats parked in a big row, each parked side by side. Abdul met me at the dock and picked me up in a Kashmir style canoe, which he paddled me out to the houseboat in. He stood up in the front of the boat as is the style over there. "They would be efficient at stand-up paddle boarders!" The water was brisk, as it had just finished being winter. Abdul had a butler who would help the guests out with whatever they needed. We tied onto his houseboat and I climbed up the latter to enter my quarters. It was eloquent! Great Kashmiri rugs draped on the walls in each room. There was a kitchen, a living room, a bedroom and a bath. Abdul pulled out a hookah bong so we could all have a smoke to get us started. He called it the hubbly-bubbly! The bowl was filled with Kashmiri tobacco, and then he made a paddy of fine Kashmiri hash with his fingers. Back then my lungs were not conditioned to smoking weed like they are now, so the bong made me choke when I took a smoke. Undoubtedly, I was a one hitter quitter as tobacco tears my lungs up, and I never smoked anything other than weed and twice Salvia. Being high on that houseboat with the realization of where I was, so far away from home and everything I was familiar with made me feel like an ant that willingly drifted out of his colony and was in an entirely different ant colony where everything is different. Abdul gave me a red rubber thermos to fill with hot water, so I could sleep with it as it still got really cold at nights. "I loved it!" Everything was lavished in fine Kashmir artwork which was beautiful, but I found it too fancy and so too "shi shi". I was happy with the thought of staying at the cheapest places I could find. Plus, I knew that it was costing me more than I wanted to pay to stay there. He had caught me good. I met some friends who were also staying at the lake and I stayed occupied for about two weeks on Dhal lake before taking the long bus journey back to New Delhi, where the transit was. Kashmir's Dahl lake was only the beginning of my India journey, which would next visit Rishikesh and the famous Himalayan Pilgrimages, McLeod Ganj and Dharmsala, which I also visited. I took the train to Karala in South India stopping at various Hindu sights on the way, including the desert town of Hampi in Rajasthan's desert. Hampi was filled with real gypsies, and everything was carved out of Granite stone, even the room I was staying in. Riding on the Indian rail made me humbler of a human being, as I encountered beggars who ride on the railways, begging as a means of income. On a travel on the rails, I heard the horrible "rupi" moan coming from a small mangled Indian figure with a deformity of his leg twisting backward so it is not functional. This, of course, forces him to be a beggar as a means of income. Some traveling fellows told me of the person on the train with the foot deformity that it was rather common for parents to deliberately cause their child's foot to grow deformed by keeping it in a bucket at a young age, giving him a deformity but also a career for the whole family: ma and pa. The diarrhea I got in India from eating foods that were cooked by local street vendors and drinking from a local water source one time at the beginning of my trip in an ashram in Rishikesh completely drained my bowels. I met Teddy, from Australia, Anna from Argentina and (Lady Swami) from Mexico/California, all whom I had encountered my first dead body with. So peaceful was the sight, a sai babba sit on a bench by the Ganges motionless, with flies invading the air around him. His mouth was slightly opened. I traveled with Teddy and Anna to Dharmsala, to the home of the Dali Lama, where they caught sight of him loading into his vehicle (I put my head down, so I didn't see him.) Love/hate, India was amazing/disgusting, and it pushed me in more ways than one, shaping me for four and a half months to be strong enough to overcome all the hardships that I must endure to overcome rat lungworm disease.

Me after my India trip, living in Berkeley CA. had lost 30+lbs

5
Bahamas to Puerto Rico (solo)

Puerto Rico was my last travel before I moved to Hawaii, but first I stayed with family-Greg and Patty (my aunt and uncle) in Freeport Bahamas. There, I freed dove and kayaked in the beautiful turquoise water. The vis underwater was over a hundred feet where you look at live, colorful coral reef that was actually fifteen feet tall when you swim down to them. They didn't seem so large when you \are floating at the surface. It was sixty feet down to reach the sand pockets which are between coral patches. The place we usually dove was called Papa Dock, which was a sunken tugboat at a depth of thirty-five feet. My uncle Greg and I kayaked out to the reef where Papa Dock was, and Greg would take a line down to the sunken tugboat and tie it off, then we would hook our crafts together so they would not drift with the current. We did breathe up's, where you pack your lungs with as much air as you can for fifty breaths, hyper oxygenating our lungs. This allowed us to be able to hold our breaths for long enough to swim through the windows of the wreck. Eventually, on a trip I took to Bimini on a dive boat full of scuba divers, as the free diver deckhand comes along guy, I free dove every sight we visited. I ate meals with them, cooked by the Aussie named Joel, and we also made a lot of PB and J's together. Eventually, I got the opportunity to follow a mooring line down to the bottom where it was tied to the bow of a sunken ship. Our sail boat's depth finder said that the ocean floor was seventy-five feet down. Satisfied with my new record, I surfaced feeling a bit like the world-famous diver Jacque Cousteau. My friend, Tommy Thai-boxer, or Tom is an English bloke from Fairy hill England who lives in Freeport Bahamas and dives with reef sharks for tourists in his job at Unexo. He can put a shark in a trans and then balance the creature, elongated on its nose, and he held it with each palm. He has even balanced one with each hand, but first, he sets one up to balance on his head. So, he has three sharks, each separately balancing on his body.

Me swimming to the sharks

6
Puerto Rico

After my travels were complete, I wanted to settle down somewhere where it was warm, and the surf is good. I was twenty-one years old, and I had already visited Bali and around in Indonesia, India, Bahamas and now Puerto Rico. Puerto Rico was my last venture Before Hawaii, and it was the waves that I was in pursuit of not the culture. Domes was the most frequent surfing spot I surfed at, as it was just a half mile walk down the hill on a trail. A big white dome structure marked this site as "Domes." The surf was sick in Rincon, so that's where I stayed. You could get these grilled turkey-melts sold by a Purto Rican lady that were sufficient surfer food. It consisted of three nearby breaks which I would visit, Dombs, Tres Palmas and Dog mans. I stayed at a Puerto Rican man named Tony's house. He had all vacant rooms for rent which were each decorated with seashells and other knickknacks. "Junk" was glued to the walls of his entire compound artistically! Tony was a real character-he'd always address himself in third person and spell his name out when doing it, "T-O-N-Y, if you ever need help, just ask Tony!" There were cats all over his compound, and he addressed them all as "Mish." He lived alone because his wife and kids were in NYC, where they lived in a large Puerto Rican community. Tony liked it better living in Puerto Rico, so he stayed there. I would practice Spanish with him as he made moonshine with his two buddies "Curly and Moe."

I decided to move to Hawaii instead of going back to mainland California where I had family. I also decided to move to Hawaii where I also had family. I flew back and stayed with my cousins, Amy and Jerry Slay in Fort Lauderdale Florida, Jerry whom I had met on the trip for the first time in the Bahamas and we were 'automatic' fond of each other. In the Bahamas, we surfed long, glassy waves on one sunny, windless Bahamian morning. We also went lobster spearing (when it was still legal to do so.) We speared like fifteen lobsters and cooked them all up for dinner with Greg and Patty. In Fort Lauder dale Jerry and I shredded through his sister Amy's suburban neighborhood, leaning a piece of plywood against trees and using it as a bank for our skateboards. I was the first one to reach the top and then doing a 180 degree turn around and come back down and ride it out. That's because I was a more experienced skater, but it didn't take Jerry long to pick it up and shred at the skate park in Pahoa. Jerry didn't enjoy the suburban lifestyle he was living, so we decided to move to Hawaii together; he wanted to be somewhere out of the city where he could grow weed, and I enjoyed his companionship. He had like a thousand bucks saved up from working at "Arturo's Pizza joint," and so he decided that he was going to move to Hawaii with me on the second day of my visit with them. I stayed with them for a week, so it was a quick choice on his part.

When we got to Wah-wah's jungle in Hawaii, the road was gravel except for a hill that they paved right in front of Lyn and Geoff's house so that cars could climb it. That's where we first stayed when we moved to Hawaii is in the basement of my aunt Lyn and uncle Geoff's farmhouse. Later, we moved back to the tent. We were obligated several hours of farm work per day for exchange for our stay. Eventually, we got $10 an hour grunt groundwork from the local jungle neighbors, Dallas and Beverly. We would often drink a beer and make guakamole after work with them. Evenings are so divine in Hawaii. We would go outside in our new "always warm humid environment" and would rip down the entirety of that cement strip, rolling onto the gravel with our skateboards.

Me swimming crazy Cuban style (no fins) at Papa Doc (a sunken tug-boat) a frequently dived site we free dove, with a depth of 35 feet.

Me penetrating the tug's window.

7
Ratlung Man

Hi I'm Graham McCumber. I am thirty-two years old now, but when I got rat lungworm disease I was twenty-four. My case was severe, where I went into a three-month coma. At one point, my mom was given the option to pull the cord on me because they thought I would not make it, but by an act of defiance, I lived. The medical protocol for ratlung is high doses of steroids. This is to make your body's immune system strong enough to fight off the ratlung parasite. Then the anti-helmetic's (anti-parasitic): Ivor-mecton and El-bendazol are administered, but that is a controversial subject. It is agreed upon that if you were to kill a large load of parasites and the dead bodies remained in "let's say the brain," that this would cause inflammation and further infection. The ratlung parasite can live for years in the body though, so if your body's own immune system cannot fight off the invading forces, then if you were not to take a horrible poison to kill them, they would continue eating at your brain. "I think, better dead than alive eating my brain!" I was questioned shortly upon awakening from the coma what I thought happened. My response was "I crashed at the skate park?" When they said that I got a rat lungworm parasite and that's what put me in the coma, recall began to occur. Suddenly, the memories of me being sick in my Kapoho house, then going to stay with Lyn and Geoff flooded back.

Coming out of the coma brought into a surreal state where imagination and pre-coma thoughts blended with present actual reality, changing it to what my mind saw as tangible. I saw many things during my hospital visit that were not really happening. For example, I thought the stuffed animals that my mom had bought for me at the hospital's souvenir shop, "Tiggy (the tiger) and Monkey (the monkey) were real. One day I looked at the Tigers' paw and said to my mom, "wow he is going to be BIG when he grows up!" I thought they were both a continuation of the real cat's that I had in Kapoho, Mitten and Soley's cat." Repeatedly, I mistook the hospital room for my old cabin in Kapoho. This surreal state lasted about two or three weeks until I recognized them as stuffed animals. Another time is shortly after I awoke from the coma and my boss (ex), Bob Kirk came to the hospital to visit me. When he walked in I saw a little boy with him that was entirely blue and naked (except for a loin cloth). I said, "who's the little boy?" His reply with a baffled face and a smirk, "what boy?" I'm quite sure it was "Krishna," in child form.

Early on I was in a flood of emotions because I thought my legs were paralyzed. My PT, Robert says "they're not paralyzed Graham, look you're moving them right now, all you need to do is strengthen them. Then you will walk again." I saw this was True, so from that point on I was determined to walk again. At twenty-four, after the coma, I was too weak to sleep on my belly because I was unable to roll myself over to my back, where I would be stuck. I was truly the weakest link! Weak on the outside but uncannily strong on the inside, I went to the mental gym to begin the physical transformation that I would soon begin to undergo. My body was atrophied, and I was a quadriplegic when I came out of the coma. Rendered unable to shower myself, I was taught how to shower myself again. I even had to get help cleaning up my poo; only they call it "bowel movements" (BM.) When first awakening from the coma, I was unable to talk because my vocal chords were so badly damaged in the insertion and then removal of the trach. After the breathing-tube was taken out and replaced with a fenestrated trach which allowed me to talk again, my first words were, "Luke, I am your father." I chose to say that because I knew that my voice would be mono toned, like a smoker who lost their vocal chords, so I thought it would be funny for me to say with a robotic voice/Darth Vader voice. I also obtained a fart machine while in the hospital which brought me tremendous amusement and joy.

When we were released from the Hilo Hospital, we went to Lyn and Geoff's farmhouse in Wah-wah, a place where I once lived during my very first venture to Hawaii at seventeen. This basement room was also the first place Jerry and I stayed when we arrived in Hawaii in 2005. There was/still is very much undeveloped jungle there and we were in the midst of it. I had to start very small when I came to my senses, which happened gradually upon my being released; my mom got me to start from crawling, then I raisedfenestrated myself to sit on the couch with tricep strength. My muscles were conditioned by my prior days as an athlete, and being physically fit and active since high-school was an asset to me. So, though a cripple, I was innately strong. I went from being an enthused surfer with a strong surfing stoke (desire to surf) in my life prior, to being sedentary because of my injury. Before I even tried using any walking sticks to adjust my balance when walking, while staying in my aunty Lyn's basement in the jungle of Wah-wah, I feebly walked from the couch to bed and back, plopping gracelessly down each time. I was exhilarated to have just accomplished the feat of walking across an open plain of space unsupported, because let me tell you, "a walker is limiting, and just sucks!" I felt accomplished being erect on both feet and making those six steps from bed to the couch. Now I was ready for the walking sticks, so my mom went into the jungle to fetch me two guava sticks of adequate length and girth for me to use as walking sticks. So, for now on I would do all my walking with the sticks and was determined to rid them. Every morning I would go on walks with my mom down the gravel road but first our walks stayed in the yard though, and I would have to rest every twenty feet. Quickly twenty feet became thirty feet and so on. The food that we were preparing for meals was quality food, often grown on the land or near-by. I had a mostly whole food diet and drank green/spirulina smoothies every morning before the walks on the gravel road, which eventually went all the way to a destination called "Honolulu landing", which is a gravel pit-Iron wood forest that overlooks the great ocean from its tall cliffs, and is over a mile from the farm. It's also called "Sand pit", and the dirt bikers used to use it as a riding area before they got kicked out. These daily walks played a huge role in my recovery speed says Dr. Allen Thal from Hawi, who recommended that I walk every morning. It was here that I learned how to ride a bike again by charging a grass hill and crashing at the bottom. I was doing ground workouts at home as well and we went to the Pahoa pool where I practiced walking in the shallow end with weights on my legs. This was to develop repetitious muscle memory. We treated ourselves with an ice cream cone from the gas station as an extra motivational incentive. Early on, exercise was essential for me to do. It was most beneficial then because that is when the body is most efficiently shaped back into form if it has been extraordinarily damaged and disc-shaped like mine was. My body had become quite out of alignment while I laid motionless for three months in that hospital bed. You must shape yourself early on, and constant proactivity goes along the lines with proper nutrition as key in recovering from neurological injuries. This is because the brain has recently been found to have plastic-like properties which can heal from injuries by building new pathways if the proper nourishment and the routine exercise are given. This is also because the formation of our bodies is natural, hence from nature. Nature has the innate life-force energy giving it the ability to repair from even the most severe devastations. This is our God energy, or lifeforce energy.

Slugs hide in vegetation, especially when it is wet outside, so inspect your vegetables while preparing meals, before consuming it.

8
My prayer to a full moon

I have been a Truth seeker for what feels to be, "my whole life!" That's why I went to India, and I did feel more humble and wise when I returned. But did not satisfy my quest for Truth. And so:

I had just headed home from a couple of friend's house eleven o'clock some night in December of 2007. I drove my pickup down the bumpy, cinder road to the main road "red road." The moon was brighter and fuller than any moon that I remember ever consciously fixating my eye on. God is in everything natural, and that is why my prayer worked so powerfully. The moon is a naturally created object that is so unfathomably distant from us, 238,900 miles, and I knew that when you fixate on a natural object such as a stone or a flower, because God is in every natural thing, then the full moon would be the perfect object to fix my gaze upon to connect with God. I got out of my truck on the side of the road and raised my head up to the radiant glow of the moon. I prayed for truth and clarity of life. I knew that in order to receive that truth would require me to endure a hardship of some sort, but I felt ready to overcome a severe injury and reverse the damage that it caused. If that is what it would take to give me the humbleness I wanted, which would also give me more compassion, to myself and others, then that was what I wanted. Though I did not specify what the injury would be, with impeccability I specified that though I would experience being handicapped, that is not how I would remain. I prayed that it would make me a happier, stronger, all compassionate-wise human being, and when I overcame the hardships, it would shape me into the best of my potential. The experience would make me ready to be a lover, to myself then to another. I so badly wanted to experience a lover, yet I was afraid to truly express myself and my feelings. The truth is, I did not honestly know myself, and so there is no way I could truly love myself. You must first love yourself before you can love another and there was a point that I didn't love my life-experience or myself where I was. I now-again understand and love my life experience and self. I see so many young couples, but I wonder "how many of them actually love themselves? Do they really love their partner?" So, my prayer was to make me feel ready to embark with another soul. Another request I wanted out of the prayer was to be united with my healing powers. I wanted to be a healer. I was at that point aware of the one dysfunction that plagues most human beings on earth, which is the ego. The ego is the trickster inherent in all humans which direct circumstances affect the manner in which we perceive and live our lives. It is the false I who is not whom you actually are. The ego is just a part of the human condition that we're supposed to have consciousness over to not listen to it and be deceived by it.

I began saying my prayer and was feeling so ready to accept the challenge I was calling to myself so that I could evolve to the place that I wanted to be. I wanted to be at a place of fearless compassion and self-love. I could feel God's universal presence in the bright moon and could also feel my prayer being heard by God, so I knew that my prayer would be granted. That is what I trusted, and I kept that trust even throughout my deformity when I looked and moved like Frankenstein. My movements were all jerky and spastic due to the ataxia I had early on after leaving the hospital, because of being comatose for so long. It was not until 2013, five years after ratlung, that my ataxia went away, and my energy began to return, with the consistent attend of acupuncture. My recovery has been a multicausality; I was proactive from day one, by going to the mental gym (you actually can get stronger by just putting your mind's attention there,) instead of dwelling in negativity.

9
Word about me from the mom

An MRI showed worm tracks in his brain, a left side empyema, hydrocephalus, post encephalitis brain atrophy, and history of eosinophilic meningitis complicated with severe demyelinating encephalitis, and cachexia. Shortly after he developed hospital-acquired infections including methicillin-resistant Staphylococcus aureus (MRSA), pneumonia, and Clostridium difficile, and damage to the 6th cranial nerve resulted in diplopia. The patient ran a persistent fever, and a CAT scan revealed a pleural effusion. The patient was flown to Honolulu for a video-assisted thoracostomy including decortication for persistent empyema. An MRI determined he had communicating hydrocephalus and he was declared to be in a persistent vegetative state.

The family requested the administration of supplements, which included spirulina and chlorella, curcumin and noni (Marinda centifolia), as well as the Chinese herb Xing Nao Wan, which was shown in a similar case in China to be effective. Additionally, acupuncture treatments were initiated. While his condition was reported as grave with a dismal prognosis and not hope of much recovery, seven weeks after hospitalization the speech therapist began working with the patient, and by nine weeks he was able to chew and swallow ice chips, nod yes and no, laugh, and grip hands. Progress continued with the patient beginning to breathe through normal airways and move his hands. Within three months after hospitalization physical therapy began, the tracheal tube was changed to a fenestrated tracheal tube, and the patient's status was downgraded. Shortly after the patient spoke for the first time and was able to converse in short sentences. The paresthesia had generally subsided, replaced by numbness, and he had lost the use of two fingers on his left hand. His short-term memory was greatly impaired; however, his long-term memory was intact. His gaze was deconjugate with some nystagmus present, and he had severe ataxia, some hallucinations, and insomnia. Over the course of the month, his swallowing reflexes improved, and he was able to eat and drink. Four months after hospitalization he was able to walk with a walker and assistants and was released.

After hospital release, the victim's symptoms included conditions mentioned above and loss of core strength, inability to walk without assistance, loss of balance, double vision, spastic voice and breathing, difficulty with bowel and bladder functions, insomnia, insufficient energy. Upon release from the hospital, additional supplements were added which included EPA/DHA, Acetyl-l-Carnitine, Vitamin B1 (benfotiamine), and B12 (methylcobalamin.) Acupuncture treatments continued. Four months after hospital release the patient began intravenous vitamin therapy consisting of doses of phosphatidylcholine and glutathione alternated with high doses of vitamin C plus B vitamins and trace minerals, delivered as an IV drip. His recovery, while painful and slow, has been steady, and he is able to participate in many activities, though more than eight years later he still has symptoms typical of acquired brain injury. In light of the dim prognosis given at the onset of the disease, this case demonstrates the ability to recover functionality from serious neurological damage from RLWD if proper treatment and support is given, and speaks to the potential importance of non-traditional therapies for recove

10

Sheri Thal

"My voice/music teacher"

It was soon after the hospital that I first went to Sheri Thal's house down Kolole drive, just down the Kings highway from Hilo, towards Lyn and Geoff's farmhouse in Wah wah. Sheri lives towards Hilo from Hawaiian Paradise park HPP subdivision. Kolohe and HPP are two roads of subdivisions heading makai (seaward) from the Highway heading to Pahoa and Kalepana. When my constipation began after the hospital and so mum, and I drove almost two hours, all the way to Hawi to see Dr. Allen Thal, who is the natural path that recommended me to take buffered vitamin C for my constipation, and he told me to walk every day to aid my recovery. While we were there, he assessed me, and could notice the quiver that my voice had, which was very pronounced at that time. This is because not too long before that my vocal cords were lacerated in the insertion of a tracheostomy for my coma. That's what I thought, but when I read this to my mom, she says it is because of a different reason, so no laceration Truly occurred. Dr. Thal told us that his daughter, Sheri Thal is a voice coach and that it would be a good idea for me to start voice lessons with her. We agreed, and we contacted Sheri and I started my first lesson, which I enjoyed immensely. Before ratlung, I played guitar and sung remakes "Graham style," which sounded completely different from the original but had its own enjoyable style. Before ratlung, I had talent playing "my favorite songs to play" when I played by myself. I was afraid to express my vocal abilities in front of others though. I was afraid to let myself sing fully for I feared of other's criticism on me. The fear constricted my vocals, which disallowed me to sing to my full potential, "which is actually quite remarkable!" Because of being afraid of expressing my True full voice, I sucked when trying to play for people. I sometimes would feel anxious if there was a guitar sitting around when I went to a hang-out session with people involved because I thought I might be asked to play a song. I really wanted to play, but I had to much fear to be musically self-expressive. I was singing along with Tom Petty's "Free fallin" and Eagles "Hotel California" at our first lesson, not holding back at all. It was so fun, and then I found out that Sheri played guitar too, so we started guitar and voice lessons from there.

For the first three years, we played remakes. I never once held back! This is because ever-since ratlung I seldom let fears get in my way from achieving what I want, especially insecurity fears. Now, I stay rooted to security by the self-realization of my own divinity. I wrote numerous songs with Sheri, who taught me how to be a songwriter. From then on, it was originals all the way. She used to come to my house for music lessons that we had at my kitchen table. In the beginning, it was a lot of voice drills that she had me do, such as "sirens" and all kinds of voice exercises to strengthen my vocals and make me proficient at singing in different ranges and pitches. Those were done at her house in HPP. Later, I was into open mic, and I would go when I could get a ride, because it goes until late at night and it gets too dark for me to safely ride my bike there. I did a few times though. Also, because open mic is always at night and since ratlung, I have been too tired to play past nine o'clock anyways. I really liked it when Sheri played her piano notes from low to very high, and I matched it with my voice. One singing game we did was I sing: "The lips, the teeth, the tip of my tongue," stepping up in musical notes each time she played the piano as I sang it. I really enjoyed doing falsetto or hitting the high notes. Sheri and Bub Prat held recitals every so often with their music students. I loved it, always playing originals! The most recent song that I wrote was a love song to Madison, an amazing, beautiful divine feminine light being whom I met and have real strong feelings for! I am convinced that she is an indigo child born to spread light in this world, and one day we will join and amplify each other's light. But like in the lyrics I wrote in her song, "allowing what is and letting it be." Maddie girl is the name of my song to her, and I was so happy to be able to play it for her before she got on the airplane and headed home last summer. 2017 Allow an Alliance is a rap style song played with my guitar that speaks about our True divine feminine selves that each one of us possesses inside, we just need to allow ourselves to express more of it. This is the song that I chose to play at one of Bub and Sheri's recitals. I believe in medicine music that promotes healing and puts smiles on faces. I have temporarily given my songwriting up so I can write this book, but when my book is finished I will resume songriting, only this time I will learn how to play my Kahoon/box-drum and write and sing songs with that.

11

My first travel after ratlung off island to California

While I was still in the hospital, not too long after the coma, I set some goals for myself. First, I set the goals of going to California to visit family, and then to Florida so that I could retrace my path, and I would visit my hometown and friends. From there, we would go and visit my aunt and uncle, Greg and Patty, in Freeport Bahamas, where I had stayed before and free dove all summer, which was Bahamas winter. I also set the goal of going to Bali and thanking Pak Mangku and my friends and family in "the junior healing team for metaphysically healing me from a distance, only that came later-on the next trip. I was told he sucked the worms right out of my head (metaphysically from a distance.) My lifestyle shaped me into being strong enough to travel, so that's what mom and I did. We booked a flight to California where we had a reunion with my siblings and where mom and I house sat a house in the Berkeley hills with a piano and a boxer canine named Hazel. She was a big-fun lovely dog who liked to go on walks and play fetch with the whip-it stick. She struck a flame of desire in my heart for a dog. I pounded some deep soulful music on the old piano that was there and the old Kensington style house we were sitting had great acoustics to boot. I got my walking practice in by walking Hazel on the sidewalk of the neighborhood to a trail on land that was undeveloped. That's where we got to connect with nature, where there were no cars or houses, just trees, and grass skapes. Hazel was a spark that started a flame of desire for a dog in my heart. I will never forget old Haze blaze. California was only the beginning of our journey. Next, we were going further South, all the way to the Caribbean, but first Florida.

12

Florida

So, the next place we flew to was Florida, where we stayed in my old hometown of Goodland, which is a little fishing/crabbing town, where I was born and spent my early childhood. We stayed with old friends from my childhood, Ray and Amy, and their daughters, Marian and Jamie. Marian was not there though, nor was Jamie. Amy and Ray were busy working at their store, "the little bar" (which I have been to a million times when Niel, Caydie and I were young) so we just stayed at their familiar as heck house and ventured the just as recognizable town of Goodland. So, we didn't get to see much of them either. They had a dog named Zeppelin who felt like he was my dog for that week. I played fetch with him, snuggled with him in the guest bed and he made the flame of the desire to be a dog owner burn stronger. Walking around Goodland was a flashback in time; it looked mostly the same as when I was a keiki (kid,) only everything got closer together. The little town store of "Margood" used to be a biking journey for me to get to but now that I had grown up, I'd say it is no more than forty feet. It's funny how our perceptions change as we age but are eerily reminiscent.

13

Freeport Bahamas

The final and premier destination of our trip was Freeport, Bahamas, where we stayed with my uncle, Greg and Aunt Patty. Actually, we didn't stay with them. The owner of the community "Smith point" is my aunt Patty's daughter, Amy's boyfriend, Fred Smith. Fred is a lawyer, so he is very affluent and graciously let us stay in one of his colorful Bahamian style guest houses on the dock. We were right across from the "Dolphin Experience," so we got to see trainers working with dolphins daily. Dolphins would be leaping through hoops, held by their trainers across the canal from us. At night, we could hear them slapping in the water. It sounded as if someone was down on the docks firing off a handgun. Greg and Patty are dog people and at the time owned three dogs, Chai, Konan, and Yoda. Chai was an old golden retriever; he was a good old boy! Golden Retrievers tend to develop hip problems as they age so his back end was always falling over. Konan was a Bahamian pot cake (mixed mutt) that was very timid because he was a rescue dog and he had been abused in his life-prior, so he has been conditioned to fear. He was golden and handsome. Sylvia, my aunts step daughter found Yoda when she was a potcake pup lost out on the streets. She was bald and had pointy ears at her puppy age, so she looked like Yoda from "Star Wars," and that's how she got her name. She is white now. I walked them on the long white beaches with my mom. This was in 2010 when we stayed in the Bahamas, and those three dogs made the dog desire flame grow even stronger inside of me, but I had to contain it because it was not until much later in the fall of 2014 that I would get the wonderful golden dog in my life today. I attended physical therapy, which was instructed by two Bohemian PT sisters. I would go with John, Patty's senior dad that she was caregiving for. Three times a week John and I went to PT sessions.

Every morning my mom and I would bring bread down to the beach and start seagull riots. They were fairly-tame because I could hand feed them. It was the most fun interacting with wildlife on sparkly-shiny Bohemian mornings on the beach. All along the beach were uprooted Ironwood trees, roots horizontally vertical, which made perfect objects to climb. The roots allowed an area of up to twenty feet high for a climbing wall. I was tapping into my past rock-climbing days of when I used to climb at "Indian rock" when I lived in California, gripping the dried-out, dead roots strongly as I pulled myself to the top. I considered this a form of rehabilitation, making me stronger and developing muscle memory. Greg and Patty had two kayaks which I often used in the past, in the summer when I was twenty-two. I felt like I wanted to try to paddle the dolphin but when I tried to get in my ataxia overtook, and I had no stability on that narrow floating craft. I decided where we were at in that little community with virtually no traffic, was a perfect place to relearn biking. Fred had gifted us bikes to use for our trip, so I biked around the paved walking trail like it was a dirt bike track. As proof to myself that I was getting stronger, I eventually swam all the way to the canals exit. I cannot say how far it was, perhaps six plus swimming pools with no breaks. I had a mask, so I could see the terrain that was under me, mostly sand and mud. I feared not for sharks because my uncle Greg taught me that sharks are but dogs that live underwater, and like a dog, they only attack if they smell your fear. I was also not afraid of sharks getting me because they never swim up the canal, and the only kind of sharks in the area are docile reef sharks. But, there always was a fear somewhere on the edge of my mind that there was a rogue tiger shark, out of control in shallow waters for some reason. One time it was really windy and stormy out, so there was some surf kicked up in the usually bath tub flat bay at Smith-point. I wanted to take advantage of this, so I borrowed Fred's son, Seddy's surfboard and headed down to the water and cautiously paddled out. The water was murky from the storm, and the waves were much bigger than I've witnessed before that day. I was in just waist deep water getting into chest deep, and I was on my belly paddling when "wham!" Something slimy and with much force slammed my hand, jamming my thumb bad. My hand smelled like fish when I held it out of the water, and this frightened me, so I bolted. Later, when I told Greg, he said it was probably a Jackfish "but who knows?" Sharks or no sharks, the Caribbean waters added a healing element to my recovery.

14

A blue water lily, a white waterlily and a rose

"A white-water lily and a rose"

Pak Mangku is a metaphysical healer who I had met on my first trip to Bali when I was seventeen years old. I met him on three occasions in the physical form during three different trips to Bali. Although not consciously aware of it, during times when I was deep into the coma he and two other Balinese guys (both friends of mine), Lolet and pak Bayu, encountered my spirit in places other than where I was (in a hospital bed.) At several

occasions, my spirit was being seen in Bali when it was vacant from my body, because it did not want to inhabit a body as sickly as mine was, plus I really enjoyed Bali so it was a likely place for me to go if I could escape my body. While in our immediate world the perspective doctors in Hawaii were giving us was grim, negative and hopeless. Luckily, there was another source of information coming from my Aunt Jean, who was relaying messages from Bali about what was actually happening with my spirit. The messages that Jean was relaying were coming from Pak Mangku, and the team of Balinese healers, all of whom were my good friends from Bali. This information was an automatic inspiration to my mom. My mom believed this side of the story over the doctors, which filled her with hope instead of doubt. She was given instructions to collect specific flowers for melikots or ritual bathing-cleansings to give to me which are routinely performed in Bali for many different purposes, but the purpose for mine was to bring my spirit back into my body, which would essentially bring me back to life. She was told to smear honey on my lips so that I could remember the sweetness of life. For one important melilot, a white-water lily, a blue water lily, and a rose were needed to be collected. The white-water lily and the rose came easily, whereas the blue water-lily was a bit of a challenge to find. It was a group effort to find the blue water lily between my mom, my sister Caydie and my aunt, Lyn. At this point, I will turn the story over to my mom to tell because she was there and conscious of the event whereas I was not.

15

The story of the blue water lily:

My mom:

"Graham went into a coma on Tuesday, Jan. 13, 2009. We were flown to Queen's Hospital in Honolulu in an air ambulance the following day. On Thursday, we were told by a doctor that there was no hope for him. The MRI showed worm tracks in the brain, and the damage for the parasite was so great, and we should consider our choices, including helping him pass. On Friday Graham's older brother, Neil, and his sister, Caydie, flew in from California. We did not know if Graham would live, and there were big decisions to make. The doctor took us all into a room with a social worker and told us all again what they saw, and what they felt the situation was, which was hopeless. Caydie was devastated, as she was sure Graham was going to be ok. We went back into the room after the doctors finished, and Caydie and Neill stop by Graham's head and spoke with him, of love, of love, of love. And tears were falling. And then, Graham opened his eyes, for the first time in five days, and he looked right at them. I think that was when the decision was made, and it was pure love between brothers and sisters that called it. The term miracle fit the moment well. That was Saturday. On Sunday, we got the message from Bali via the junior healing team from Pak Manku. We needed to do a melikat for Graham, and we needed to use a blue water lily. We were staying at an apartment provided by the hospital on the hospital grounds and did not have a car. We had walked through parks and gardens and palaces all morning on a search for a blue water lily, but we could not find one. That evening Caydie, Neill, Bryce (Graham's very close friend from high school), and Lyn and I were sitting in the living room around the coffee table we had transformed into an altar for Graham. Graham's Buddha was on the table, surrounded by photographs of Graham through various stages of his life and with his family. We still needed a blue water lily. "How are we going to find one?" Caydie asked in a bit of despair. And Lyn replied, "First we need to imagine it." And with **that, she picked up a magazine and found a page that had the color blue on it. Deftly, she cut a tiny, blue water lily with scissors** and set it on Buddha's lap. Caydie looked down at the table and saw a note. It said, "if you need anything call me." And the name Katy and a phone number. Caydie asked who the note was from. I said I didn't know, and I thought it was from someone Lyn knew, and Lyn said the same, she thought it was for me. So Caydie replies, "well we need a blue water lily, so I'm going to call her." And she did.

It turned out the woman was going to take a class Lyn was going to teach that weekend and had to cancel because of the family crisis going on. The story was being carried by newspapers because besides Graham being in a coma from rat lungworm disease; there was another woman from the Puna/Pahoa community who was also in a coma from it at the same time. So, Caydie put two and two together and figured it was Lyn's nephew who was in the hospital in critical condition. She asked how she could help and Lyn told her we needed a blue water lily. “No problem,” she replied, “Home Depot has water lilies.” We asked how to get there by bus, and she said she would drive there herself and get one and deliver it to us with anything else we needed. The water lilies were all closed up when she got there because it was nighttime, but she pried them open and found a blue one and picked it and brought it over to our apartment and gave it to us. And that is the story of how we came to have the blue water lily for the melikat.

16

Demons before sleep

Soon after the coma, I saw creatures, like demons and grotesque visions of monsters. I have even seen what I was told to be Dorga, the Hindu Goddess who eats babies. In front of my foreground when I was laying down to go to bed at night, right before I fell asleep that is who I would see. And it was so scary and disgusting and “why would I see them?” I thought! It wasn’t just Dorga eating babies; it was also other nasty monsters like in David Boey’s “Labyrinth” only with more blood and gore. They would swipe their claws at me trying to claw my eyes out as I lay terrified on my back, on my foam pad, on the floor, in the dark. It’s like I have been a bit in fight or flight state since the trauma of rat lung. Insomnia only perpetuates my fight or flight response by jacking up my nervous system. That is what Martin says. Martin is a therapist I know from Kapoho. I began to recognize the pattern of two things about the monsters. First, they were an only illusion and could not hurt me. Second, each time they came was just before I fell asleep. In that sense, I began to enjoy the demons, like my own personal, 3D monster movie with blood and gore. I actually got a chance to have a detailed look at these creatures pretty well, "they were absolutely disgusting!" As nights went by, eventually when I realized they could not hurt me, and in fact they only appeared in the moments before I fell asleep at night, I began to like them, and soon a couple of months later when I realized I was safe and ratlung was behind me, they stopped appearing altogether.

17

Intuition/guardian angel

After ratlung's life-changing event, my once keen intuition had vanished without a trace. I was no longer able to hear it. Instead, my fears would make me follow them, and then things would fuck up. There was so much fear distracting me from Truth, and the fear kept me from seeing clearly. I was delusional because of this. One incident about two and a half years after the coma, my mom and I were swimming at Pohohiki's boat launch. I was swim/floating around with a dive mask and a snorkel, so I kept my head submerged the whole time. I was really just mindlessly drifting around to all of the familiar sandbars made of smoothened small rocks which are on either side of the boat launch, so I could stand-up. I knew that there were several boats getting ready to take off. So, at one point after some time of being underwater, I felt like I should look up and see where I was, but I ignored the feeling. That feeling was my intuition! Under a couple of minutes later I was near the dock. In fact, I was so near to the dock that I was right behind a fishing boat parked at it, about ready to back out. Before I had even lifted my head out of the water, I started feeling distortion in the water around me. My cousin, Amy Slay and her friend Julie Jay Rock were visiting us from Miami, and they were both wearing bikinis. Julie has great boobs, and Amy has a great ass! The captain and the first mate were occupied with looking at Amy's ass and Julies boobs, so they didn't notice me in the water. "Something wasn't right!" I looked up at this point to see twin engines and the boat's rear backing into me, as I was being pushed back. Suddenly the distortion stopped. I felt the propellers come to a stop while they were pressed against my inner thighs. Lucky for me my guardian angel in the form of an Opihi fisher alerted the captains of the vessel that I was in the water, so they killed the engines. When I realized what was happening, it was a terrifying feeling. I was sure there was going to be blood but no, just two cylindrical markings on either leg, just below the kneecap. When I got out of the water, and what had just happened or nearly just happened sunk in, I started crying tears of absolute terror of what could have been an appreciation for my guardian angel being present to save me from losing my legs.

I like having my hair short, but I wanted to grow it long to increase my intuition. Intuition grows in hair, and so I now cultivate it on the top of my head. I have it shaved around the sides so that I can have short hair on the bottom, which helps keep me cooler in Hawaii's hot climate. I can tie it up in a bun on the top of my head like the Buddha now like I had imagined before I grew it out. First, I had the idea of wearing my hair in this fashion; then I took the appropriate steps to ensure its completion, which is a form of manifestation. It is a pretty stylistic hair doo I will admit. Medicine for the people's Nahko bear wears this kind of haircut, and he could be a role model to me, but the original intent was not to "look cool," but to increase my intuition. A cool look is just an added benefit!

18

Banana poop on hospital floor

It was really with the introduction of solid food that my digestive system kicked back in, and I started taking solid, formed poos. Before that, it was liquid for me, and I didn't get to see it, only the nurses did who wiped my butt daily-bless their hearts, did. My GI system was a champ when I first started eating solid foods while I was still in the hospital. One day in the hospital I say to my mom, “I got to poo!” I was sitting up in my hospital bed, and so we had to do a transfer to the potty chair, which my mom mistakenly forgot to put the bucket under the toilet chair. Successful was the transfer, I did my business, but we could hear it plop on the cold floor. When we stepped back and had a look, it looked like a warm brown banana laying on the floor. It was the funniest “shit” both of us had experienced in a while, so we both laughed hysterically at the banana looking poo that I produced.

19

Suppositories

Shortly after the hospital, when my mom and I moved in with my aunt Lyn in Wah wah is when constipation began. Suddenly, my bowels froze up and would no longer make bowel movements. “This was bad!” Ratlung causes damage in the bowel track, which in turn causes horrendous constipation. My mom used to use suppositories on me when I was little and would get sometimes constipated because I was the only one not breastfed (which effects stomach flora), so she thought of it when my constipation began. It worked for gentle constipation relief in minutes. I was amazed that just by pressing a little glycerin cone in my butthole, it would produce a poo when I needed one. Suppositories only clean the end of the colon, so you cannot get a complete cleansing BM, but combine magnesium and one of those effective little buggers, and you can produce a pretty decent poo. If I had known about it earlier in life, I would have benefitted from it, as I used to remember getting constipated (mostly during my travels) and I would really not like it. Had I known that I could alleviate it by slipping a clear piece of candy corn looking thingy in my butt, I definitely would have. Not being able to poo is one contributing factor to my becoming anorexic when I was twenty-one. On days when my digestion is sluggish, I will still use one for I know how problematic blocks in the colon are for my body's overall health, and it's just annoying to have a third-jam.

20

Colonics

"colon hydrotherapy"

My colon hydrotherapist was named Susan Salas. Susan is a vibrant, radiant being that has a whole understanding of healing via having a clean colon. Each different section of the intestine corresponds to specific parts of the body. Holding feces is not what the colon is designed to do, rather with plenty of water, fiber and with strong peristalsis, the intestine is meant to rid itself of excrement daily! Feces lodged in sections of the intestine cause unbalance in the corresponding body parts. Mom drove me to colonics in Kehena. A black cat on a sign marked her driveway, which was just before uncle Robert's (the grocery store in Kalepana.) She had converted a house into her colonics business, which was quite popular. The living room was the waiting room for clients. There was often a number of people waiting to be seen. The bathroom is where the colon hydrotherapy took place. Right over the toilet is where the chair that you lay down on your back and take a crap is. So, it's basically a chair that you are sitting reclined in, like a dentist chair which is for a number of reasons, but primarily so that she could massage my belly, massaging my intestines while the process occurred. There was a five-gallon bucket of body temperature warm, alkaline water which she administers into my butthole with a long narrow tube that gravity fed into my colon. As the water reached deeper into my colon, different meridians were cleared until after the two-week session my entire colon was cleaned. As the water was absorbed into my body through my intestines, Susan massaged my belly in a clockwise direction, always making sharp jiggling motions as a means of breaking up stuck poop. She would massage clockwise because that is the same direction in which digestion occurs. She said that she could feel the difference as she worked and so did I as my belly became more flat and slender. I had to alter my diet to a vegetable soup, dahl and quinoa diet so that the food I ate during that two-week session was easy to pass through my body, leaving me with a clear GI tract. The two-week session combined with the diet alternation cured my constipation issue. She was good at spotting out the many parasites that would come out with my crap; apparently, colons naturally harbor parasites that don't hurt you! You could say that Susan and I are both anal about the cleanliness of our anuses.

21

Pterodactyl shit-spray/giant "Shart"-spray

About two to three months after the coma is when my shitter seized up and suddenly, I got really constipated. "This was a real problem; I love taking shits and having a flat belly!" How is a body to undergo healing when it cannot rid itself of simple bodily waste? It felt awful knowing that my belly was full of poo and no matter how hard I tried I could not rid my bowels of it. Dr. Allen Thal in Hawi suggested that I used buffered vitamin C. This gave me diarrhea and tremendous flatulence. He said that it was better if it was diarrhea than nothing coming out at all. I agreed! So, one night after having been taking the buffered vitamin C for some time, I awoke from sleep and diarrhea almost exploded out of my ass! I quickly jumped up from my foam pad on the floor and darted through the darkness into the bathroom. This was around 2:00 AM, so this was not usual for me to do. We had a composting toilet, so your crap went into a five-gallon bucket, then you cover your poo up with raw sawdust (not kiln dried) and close the lid. There was a toilet seat lid that you had to open on the toilet that covered the hole too. So, there was the toilet seat to open, and the bucket had to be opened as well. I was in such a hurry to sit down and explode that I forgot to take off the bucket lid. I ripped the seat up and sat down. So relieving, and almost successful! I felt the shit spray on the backs of my legs though. I got up and looked at what had just occurred. At this point, I was wearing a headlamp. Suddenly, my little kitten-cat Cinta (Chinta) pranced in, and her eyes became wide like flying saucers. Quickly she bounced off, never to sleep in my bed again and forever to be repulsed by me! It looked like a pterodactyl did a flyby shitting on the floor. "Oh great!" I did not have the heart, nor the nerve to wake my poor mom, who was my caregiver. So, I got on my hands and knees and very adroitly, bit by bit, I quietly worked at cleaning the mess up, trying not to wake my mom. I don't really know how I did It, but I made that bathroom look like nothing happened without waking my mom. I may have been able to go back to sleep that night had I only took off the bucket lid and not had to wake myself up.

That was for diarrhea and now for the flagellants! This experience is a result of taking high doses of buffered vitamin C as well. I was laying on my foam pad bed on the floor of our cabin feeling bloated with gas. I laid on my belly because of my colon hydrotherapy lady, Susan said that if I ever had gas that was stuck to lay on my belly on a hard surface and she said this will make the gas pass. It was a hot evening, so I was naked laying on my belly waiting for a fart. My stomach was uncomfortable, and my mind was drifting somewhere in the either when suddenly, a huge fart tore out of my ass. An exploding volcano of trapped air and diarrhea was the result. It wasn't a fart at all; it was a shart! The most explosive shart with the loudest volume ever! I could see little blobs of shart landing on the floor in front of me that's how I was sure it was a shart. Humorous events like this kept spirits up in difficult times.

22

Medicine-holy smoke-Weed

-

There are four significant things that smoking marijuana helps/has helped me with, which are: depression, motivation, sleeping and being present. Recovery from serious injury makes you feel bad at a constant; you just have to get used to it and try to accept it. When you resist what is your suffering will be greater. We must just accept it, (what is) envision healing, then use conscious will choice to take the appropriate actions to promote accelerated healing. So, being depressed or bummed out can and does result from injury, that is one benefit that medical marijuana has helped me with. It is like sunshine in a bag, spreading light where it is needed. For a motivational incentive; "Something but a fanom, just one puff of the cron and I'm unstoppable." (Dr Dre) Those lyrics ring true! That is one of the medicines that I have used since my injury that has aided in my recovery for motivation; "to keep going no matter what." Don't feel like working out? Just a puff is all you need. "Maybe three!" It rolls over in all areas of life too! I have had sleep Issues ever since day one, but in the hospital, I could not get marijuana to aid my sleep, not even if it was medical. That is because it was not yet recognized as medical consumption, although there is still no medical toking allowed in the hospital. Instead, synthetic narcotics are given to sedate patients who are not able to control themselves-like they have stir crazy ADD. Nevertheless, hospital patients are dosed with these synthetic opioids daily and it will be a wonderful day when the medical system becomes more progressive and begin to allow the use of medical marijuana administration in the hospital to replace synthetics. Since ratlung, mostly long since but still sometimes, I wake up in the middle of the night at 3:00am with a burning hunger that forces me to the kitchen. I have not done this since I began taking a pharmaceutical sleeping pill-Temazepam. Many times, during these early hours I would be attacked by my mind and worries, often forcing me until tears. "My mind still tests me like this!" When I was my present self, not entwined in worries then they didn't become me. When I was first able to remain present and calm with what was going on and had been going on for years, suddenly things were not so bad. Suddenly, everything was clear, my thinking seized to impede me. I stopped worrying when I was awake in the middle of the night, but rather I witnessed and observed the worries for what they were: inorganic, mind created jumble. I was no longer afraid of them, but I had to remain present and always giving appreciation for what I did have to appreciate, like when I found something that looked appetizing for me to eat in the kitchen on a late-night food quest, or the fact that I did not have the responsibility of working a bust-ass job in the morning, or the fact that I have a kitchen to go to at all. I could be a refugee from Syria without a home because my house was blown up. This allows the universe to know that I was thankful for its creations to me, and so with my appreciation to it the universe would create me more of my inner desires. It also took me to another place; by not allowing myself to focus my attention on worries, they discontinued to exist. This is another reason to direct your mind to positive thinking. There is also a possibility that the hunger which I so often experience in the middle of the night is phantom hunger, which does accompany brain injury-the gut-brain connection is affected, creating phantom hunger-but I feel that it is because calories in should match calories out and only me knows the exact doings/exertions of my day, for only I am omnipresent with my reality and I know that I am burning a lot of calories throughout the day. Finally, whenever my mind would drift from the present moment, which would pull my energy, taking one ceremonious bong hit would bring me clarity and put me in the present. This would allow me to continue with my daily tasks and chores with more ease and enjoyment. Those are the ways that medical weed has helped me and a justification that weed is indeed a medicine.

For some people, taking a toke will make them feel so comfortable that they pass out (they'll fall asleep or just zone out) but it does depend on the kind of pot too. It also depends on your current body state; if you feel tired than the tiredness will be felt more strongly. For others, it will make them paranoid, self-conscious and uncomfortable, but the type of weed you are smoking makes a difference because it can be just right too! There is Indica, and there is Sativa; Indica is the more widely grown of the two. The buds are tighter and denser on the Indica, and it offers more of a body high than sativa, which makes it better of the two for sleeping. Smoking sativa will get you higher in the head and make you feel like doing projects, which is perfect for motivation, like working out. I would be sure to separate the two for this reason. Before I knew that there was a difference in the effects of the two and I smoked some Sativa one night before bed, my mind was going into tangents and keeping me up for hours. Indica is felt upon the whole body by relaxing it, whereas with Sativa effect is felt in mind, by giving you glowing ideas and insights. "This is not wanted for sleep!" There is also a hybrid of the two when Sativa and Indica are cross bred.

I have had a habit of making offerings to the divine mother since my first trip to Bali at seventeen; the experience resonated with me so well. I have had times in my life after Bali where I made offerings regularly/daily because of the youthful experience. I started to get pretty regular with them after rat lung; once I got my bearings because I know how much impact prayer can make in one's life. I now make them daily, very seldom showing them inattention. Weed has helped me immeasurably with motivation, that is why it is always an object of sacrifice when I make offerings; it is something of value to me and in fact is an important medicine that keeps my sanity intact. Without it, I would fail to get my offerings done most of the time. That's also why I offer a bud every time I make offerings. "It is my 'holy smoke.'" Created in nature by the divine creator, paka'lo'ihi (weed) has its place in this world's medicine realm. Consuming some "holy smoke" was like a catalyst for me for making offerings. I'd smoke some weed and the idea to make offerings would just come to me, like a productive use of my time. I appreciate how the 'holy smoke' medicine leads me to continue my communication with God.

23

Supplements

I have taken a growingly complex array of supplements and superfoods such as spirulina and Chlorella, which were being pumped in my stomach peg three times a day during my coma, on word of my mother. The first supplement that I remember having profound effects on me was called “Nerve support formula,” which I started taking shortly after the hospital. It is a blend of complex B vitamins, which there are twelve of, B1 through B12. B vitamins are vital in energy production and I could notice a dramatic increase in energy, both physical and mental after a week of taking it. I also had better balance as a result of taking this complex B vitamin supplement. The bottle directed me to increase by a pill per week, starting with one a day, upping by an additional pill each week. After one-month, you just stay at four pills. This was just after I spent all that time relearning how to walk in the pool with weights on my legs and walking to Sand Pit with my mom and two guava sticks for balance back at my aunt and uncle’s jungle house in Wah-Wah. Taking certain supplements like DHA fish oils and curcumin Turmeric would ward off headaches and keep the joint pain down as my left knee was often inflamed, as result of old injuries from high school wrestling. Head-aches are also very occurrent when you have under-went ratlung.

The most often sought out supplements I would be after are sleeping supplements and pooping supplements because those were my biggest dilemmas. I have tried all the sedatives and laxatives out there, and I stick to the ones I best liked, which are the more natural ones (not pharmaceutical.) Although I am taking a Pharmaceutical pill called Temazepam for sleeping, generally Pharms are just too inorganic and not naturally created, and the adverse side effects of them are just too many for me to want to ingest into my body. The naturally occurring magnesium hot beverage that I drink in the mornings to ensure that my poo is fulfilling is just like the buffered vitamin C that I was recommended to take by Dr. Allen Thal from Hawi at the onset of my recovery. It does not have any effect on peristalsis, or the muscular wave-like action the intestines make to expel feces (which would be a laxative) but rather works as a stool softener, making the poo easier to flow from the butt.

Some other supplements of interest to me were Pycnogenol, or PBE-Pine Bark Extract, which is from a French Maritime pine tree. There was also ALC Arginate, which is a naturally existing amino acid that makes proteins inside the body. I can no longer find ALC arginate from my current Town because Hilo seems not to hold this product, but they do have L-Arginine however at Island Naturals Hilo, which is also an Amino builder, so I get that. All these supplements are for increasing blood flow, making vascular dilation reach full potential throughout the body. These were all crucial supplements for me to take as my blood flow was weak during my recovery. When one of my acupuncturist, Robby Wade searched for my pulse, it was almost not existent. Undergoing a serious injury such as a devastating car wreck, which causes you to have acquired brain injury ABI, or a parasitic infection that attacks the brain, also giving you ABI, requires you to bring your energy level back to normal, and it takes a lot of time in order to function well and completely again. Because my body was now required all this extra energy for the repair of the damage it was then faced to fix; my total body energy was depleted. I was so lucky to have a girlfriend early on when I was still extremely mangled because out of loneliness for a divine feminine lover I prayed for one, and my authentic prayers are always granted. I was blessed to be able to express my sexual nature with her, because since her and before her in fact, it has been quite the dry spell. My weak blood flow posed a problem in my new God-given situation though. Because my body was healing from ratlungs devastation, it required much energy to be utilized for my body energy to generate healing, which gave me erectile dysfunction ed. This was much less pleasurable to my partner and was really frustrating for me too. I took it harder on myself as she was such a sweetheart to me and understood that I was healing and so my body needed the energy for repair, and I knew too. When we were five minutes into intercourse, my erection would start to go limp. It self-infuriated me but it wasn't my fault, so it did not make sense to remain angry, rather accept it and imagine healing. It was then not long until I took proactivity and found the amazing blood building herbs which I talked about. The PBE is a little brown speckled, round/flat pill that is potent for its size, which I would often mix and match any of all. This would result in me popping a tremendous boner that caused a much more impactful effect on both of us.

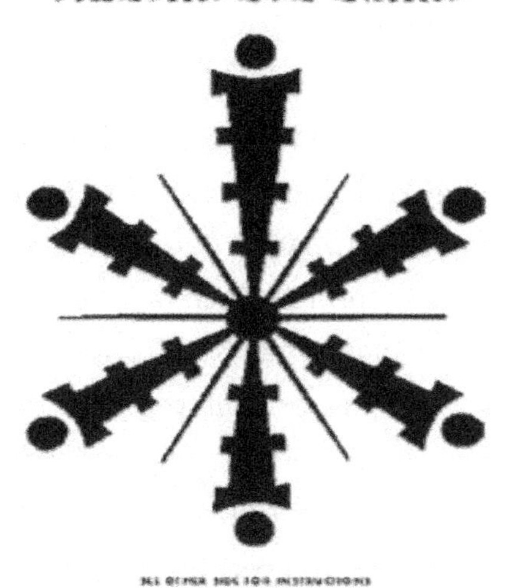

24

Tibetan Eye chart

Nerve number six was damaged in my left eye, making it crank far inside to the right. My pupil was shoved all the way to the inner edge of my eye, making a large portion of eye white exposed. This gave me an immense double vision. A friend named Karen loaned me a mechanical device with little green and red lights that light up, and you were to fixate your view on and over time it was supposed to make a difference, but I didn't use it long enough to notice any difference. I have had double vision ever since, though now it is not nearly as severe. Still, I see an image of what I am looking at but offset and at a forty-degree angle. That's what my left eye sees; my right eye is the dominating force. That's what allows me to be still able to ride a bike. When I was being wheeled in a wheel chair by my mom through the hospital halls, at that time my double vision was so severe that it would give me motion sickness if I did not shut my eyes for the stroll. A guy named Lauren, when I was released from the hospital gifted me a laminated, full-size Tibetan eye chart. For 2000 years the people of Tibet have used this method to correct visual weakness and improve eyesight. The exercises have proved fruitful over a period. It was the lama monks who derived this kind of practice. On a twelve by an eighteen-inch piece of laminated paper is a 10-inch image of a circular blade that you are supposed to put your nose in the center, 1 to 2 inches from the chart. Then follow the outline of the surface of the **very blade edge.** Follow it all the way around, then the opposite direction. Investing a few minutes per day brings immediate results. It was not until years later that I decided to be serious with it, and last year I started using it every day. Now my left pupil almost takes on the center of my eye white and people often comment on how straight my eyes are looking.

Today, I still see tracers of the image that I am looking at just offset and at a forty-degree angle. It is translucent, so it is not solid. Looking at different images will make the double vision more or less pronounced; for instance, a very messy floor with leaves where I had to spot something out in the leaves would be a confusing view for me. If I am tired is when the white lines in the road start twisting all over the place. With my left eye turned inward and my right eye looking straight, this is the reason for the vision bender. Luckily my right eye takes total domination and allows me to do things such as ride a bike. I feel safe riding my bike through town when I am feeling good but if I have an ailment such as a knee injury I am liable to end my journey and go home early because getting hurt is no longer an option of avail I give to myself. I can see myself driving one day when cars are more economically efficient.

25

Yoga

Christian Coyle was my first yoga teacher. Dynamic in her teaching methods, she was also my favorite yoga teacher at Balancing monkey studio. She was brought up in St Kitts in the Caribbean, and I bonded with her off-island/on island vibe. She became a friend who helped shape me into the form that I now have. She also mentored me. Rachel and Sarah, I got to give recognition also, as they are also dynamic yoga teacher babes.

I regularly attend what is called "yoga hour," which is an hour of yoga starting at twelve o'clock noon. Yoga has given me balance and coordination, training time and purpose to be more present with what is. At the beginning of yoga hour, Christian would always recite inspirational words that were always different and would be useful knowledge to use in the day. Sarah taught a dynamic strengthening practice as well. However, it was slightly subordinate to the intensity of Rachel's class, which was on Wednesday and Friday's. Sarah was the lighter practice as it would start out the week on Monday's. Sarah, Racheal, and Christian are awesome yoga teachers though!

Pretty early on, several years post rlwd, maybe four, the also dynamo, Handstand Mary Chapman did a number of training sessions in the parks of Hilo for me. We did everything from lunge walks to bear crawls, even to curtsies. She connected me to nature and tested me. She allowed me a friend to talk to about stuff that was hurting me to keep inside. At one session we had at the park across from the civic center, we climbed in the big banyan tree. My fear of heights has been quite exacerbated ever since ratlung, so climbing big trees was no longer my forte. She scaled right up it like a graceful spider monkey. Though I was fearful of the height, I felt safe because there were many branches to cling onto and upper body strength is my forte. I also felt safe because I was not alone, I had my friend Mary with me; even if I had to pay her for her time, it was still very enjoyable. Plus, I understood that she needed compensation for her time she spent on me. In this fastening world, it is difficult to get a cheap meal that will nourish you, so it was crystal clear she needed reimbursement for her time spent with me.

Mary taught a handstand workshop at the old balancing monkey studio, hence “handstand Mary.” Inside of the big tin shed, she taught a group of people workouts to warm us up to be ready to stand inverted. Somewhere after mid-session rain began to crash down on the tin structure making the ambient temperature of the shed cooler, also seeming to energize us. My friends Varushka and Aaron were there learning handstands with me. Only I was relearning them, which I still am. I have put much time into relearning handstands since our sessions. Long ago, before ratlung I was gaining my efficiency at walking downstairs on my hands. I could go downstairs with gravity but not yet up against gravity. Today I stand by a cement wall and walk my legs up the wall then push-off. I have had a second or two freestanding. I know that with daily practice and the absence of injury that I will be free standing inverted in God's time.

26

Indonesia with mom 2011

In fall of 2010, I visited Indonesia's Bali, and then Java with my mom. We both have spent time in Indonesia on separate occasions, in different locations, and we are both very fond of it. Going to Bali was a goal that I set for myself after the coma while still in the hospital, so I could thank Pak Mangku, "which I did!". So, we first flew into Bali, where I got to visit old Balinese friends and practice using my Bahasa, which I held onto well. We stayed at Rumah Roda, the same Balinese family compound that I stayed with each time I visited Bali. It is basically unchanged each time I go back; Dadong (Balinese for grandma) is always sitting on the cool tile floor (lantai) making offerings to be used for daily worship, or temple ceremonies, or to dispel an evil spirit that is being nakal (mischievous,) while the rest of the family helps-out with running the guest house (rooms), preparation and catering to the restaurant upstairs called Rumah Roda (wheel house), and other daily chores. Pak Darta is the respected, jolly father figure who would take tourists on rice paddy walks. Pak is short for bapak, which is a respectful way to address a man (father.) I met a golden retriever named Bruno who was another dog to build my doggy desire to push the manifestation of the dog I own today. Not a whole lot of changes accrued to the family besides the production of new little family members (Dek Gin) and accumulation of new pacar *pachar* (boyfriend/girlfriend.) Outside of the family, however, transformation in the growing town of Ubud was evident, as there was now a Starbucks Coffee shop right beside a lotus temple that was always there with no Starbucks beside it on my earlier travels to Bali.

We left Bali for a trip to Java's Tembi, where we stayed housesitting a big old house for the owner and my mom's friend, Dave Hotchner. There, we visited Gunung Merapi (fire mountain,) which is a volcano that was active and had just erupted. We were taken on the backs of motor bikes to Borobudur (a famous Buddhist temple.) It is one of those ancient stone structures made from chiseled lime stone, much like a pyramid from ancient Egypt in that they are both spectacles of glory created by man long ago (before there was modern technology.) The tourists visiting the sacred site were mostly from different parts of Java who have never encountered white people in the flesh, so my mom and I were more photogenic than the temple, which was quite annoying (because I still didn't feel good.) Java was so different than Bali. It was much less developed in Tembi than Ubud. It was like physical therapy for me being in ratlung recovery, as the sidewalks are so uneven that they can range anywhere between a half foot to two feet high within a twenty-foot stretch. Maneuvering the uneven terrain with my then unsteady balance in Java's Yogyakarta, challenged my brain to navigate those uneven places. This was excellent PT for me, and I got to do what I love to do again, which is traveling in developing countries where the people are so real and so friendly. The minds of people in developing third world countries are less conditioned with the Western concept of Capitalism than that of peoples from developed first world countries, and this is because of the social, economic status is much lower in Indo. People depend on each other and worship a higher source together. So, they work together instead of competing like we have been taught to do in the West. In Bali, the people worshiped God under Hinduism at temple ceremonies, whereas in Java they were Muslim and did their worship in Mosques, at mosque calls. They are very different religions, as Bali is animistic, and so they recognize and worship the source energy within animals, humans being number one. In Java, God was worshiped through Mosque calls, which flood the air at four every morning on loudspeakers. The calls would come from multiple mosques in various locations. So, different calls would overlap. Muslim practitioners have a rug dedicated to making prayers in a traditional Muslim fashion, which entails touching your forehead to the ground (rug.)

Just before we were to fly back to Bali, my mom got really-sick with the flu and fever; she was lying in bed for the last four days of our time in Java's Tembi. By then, I had spent enough time in Java and was ready to head back to Bali. Mom's being sick was impeding us from going though, so I had to be proactive. I did the only thing I could think of to do. I prepared an offering with a banana leaf as a base. I placed a piece of fruit on it and brought three flowers with me and cast three prayers out to the divine creator with an incents, all pertaining to my mother's rapid recovery. It was the end of the day that I made those prayers, so it must have been night time soon after that. I looked at her laying there so sick when it was so close to when we were to leave and was wondering if we would even be able to leave in the morrow.

The next morning, I left my Barn-room to walk into the kitchen and saw mom standing there. Before I saw her, I heard her banging pots and pans around as she hung them back up on the hooks, putting dishes away. She was drinking coffee, and she said she was feeling great. I was excited to see how powerful my prayer worked. I channeled God to heal my mother!

27

231 A, East Lanikaula (old location)

When we first left Wah wah and moved to Hilo we moved into a red old plantation style cabin. It was red at the time, but now it's obviously this skank blue. The owner of the complex was an agitated mid-aged woman, quite possibly high on meth. When she walked up the stairs with us to unlock the door and allow us to look inside, she brought with her a disposable red party cup full of various keys to try on the lock. In a hurried manner, she started trying keys. If they did not work, which the first ten or so did not, she would simply toss it behind her shoulder. My mom collected them as she frantically searched. The red plywood house was probably an old sugar cane camp when the plantations were still running. The floor was painted sky blue which I loved. Underneath the house was a dirt floor and we had our clothesline strung up down there for drying our laundry. Our kitchen stove was a Coleman camping stove. The house was right on a street corner, so the cars whizzed by, ripping the air every second at times. This began early in the morning at dawn. It was so loud in fact that I couldn't sleep because of the pre-anticipation I had of the next car coming, so we went to Home Depot and got me some ear muffs. I'd call them my "ear mufflers!" This blocked all traffic noises and allowed me to feel comfortable enough to take a nap in midday, even if there was traffic. But like most of my worldly possessions during ratlung recovery-mode, eventually they broke. I built a small garden by the street corner of Mililani and Lanikaula, adjacent to my house. The deep rich soil that I put in the beds was potting soil mixed with Hamakua red soil, and of course "worm castings!" This was all encased by the lava rocks that I stacked up to make a berm. Both my mom and I only had bikes during that year, so we'd bike wherever we had to go. My mom rode an old Schwinn which is a classic that needs refinished. She did not want it to be refinished or else it may be stolen on this island of so many thieves. I swear as time and technology progress so does the anarchy of this island. The Schwinn has a metal rack on the front which you can use to carry stuff. That is how we got our first convection oven; it was too heavy to ride with it so my mom walked it home on the handle bar rack of her bike from Wal Mart. Our neighbor, Kavika was our overweight "really nice" neighbor. His lifestyle was a direct reason for his morbid obesity. I felt bad for his wife, who was South Pacific Islander. Kavik's also sold me herb. Then I started getting it from my other neighbor Jay. I also got from Christies, son, then Buddy, who would roll big jays and smoke them with me. This was all in the ghetto fabulous complex where I stayed. David Hubbard is the ex-alcoholic, revered artist in Hilo who was always in front of his canvas painting a beautiful abstract life-like scenery when I would come over to pick-up from him. Though his alcoholism was short-lived (only a couple years-later on in his life.) I am so proud of, and I admire David for beating his alcoholism by consciously choosing to discontinue his consumption of cheap beer and liquor. When I would ride my bike, or walk to his house to pick up from him he was surrounded by his marijuana plants which he called his girls or his kids, depending on what stage they were at. He would even put them in a shed room with lights and play them classical symphony. Every morning and definitely each day, somebody in one of the houses near us played shredding electric guitar riffs. His name was David Luker but we called him "guitar Dave." It was at this house where my aunt Lyn gave me twelve sessions for Dr. Dustin in his Egoscue training. The method was created by Pete Egoscue and what you do in it are what are called "E-sizes that realign the load-bearing joints of your body, essentially making you pain free. The E-sizes reshaped my body into a new person. I had a lot of pain in my left knee from an old wrestling injury and so Dr. Dustin directed that I do inner and outer thighs and other E-sizes to alleviate my knee pain. It addresses the root problem by strengthening associated muscles. Egoscue was momentous in my functional recovery, and I first began to practice it at my 331 B East Lanikaula residents. Thank-you-Lyn!

A drawling of me, livin a ghetto fabiolus life in Hilo HI

28

221 B West Lanikaula (new location)

221 B, West Lanikaula, like all wonderful creations in life, was God sent for my mom and me. Not only are we far from the street, but there are also no neighbors on three sides of us. It has been so amazing being in a house with so much nature, surrounded by greenery, and far from the street. The yard is perfect for growing plants in as Hawaii boasts an ideal growing place for all varieties of flora, so I started several gardens while we have lived in this house. Inside of the house is the living room with our rooms on the far side from the front door and a deep three-step stairway going down to the kitchen, where I sit in my kitchen chair and do my studies at the computer, which I set up on the table. My mom set up a hand rail going down the deep three steps for me to hold on to, so I didn't bust my ass coming down the stairs when I was farther back in my recovery. The house is right in front of a church, "The church of Holy Apostles," where I do many various exercises in the parking lot, which has

been a fundamental exercise/recovery station for me.

It is also a perfect place to own a dog, so Hebat came out of the ethers for me there. He was my, and still is my service dog, I had to do some work to get him though. I made a GoFundMe video with my friend Arthur Dodge which raised eleven thousand (plus) dollars. That was enough money for me to fly to California and get Hebat, and also fund John, Sue McNaught and Hebat's drive to California from Rock Chester New York, where they met me, and we all flew back to Hawaii together. Hebat is my service dog, and Sue (the trainer) attended the first week of classes at UH Hilo with me and Hebat. Hebat became the revered mascot of school, and everybody knew and loved him. Hebat is totally a chick magnet as so many girls were in love with him and wanted to take him home. Hebat magnifies my spectacular self, and we also reflect each other's glory back at one another, as his golden fluff matches my blond locks.

29

HEBAT

My aunt Beth McCumber is a dog breeder; she breeds and trains dogs, golden retrievers to be more specific. She also has dog trainers who work for her, and it was her trainer, Sue McNaught, from Rockchester New York who trained Hebat into being the fine working dog he is today. One day, my aunt Beth found it in the kindness of her heart to donate one of her golden retrievers's as a service dog to me. I think it was an email that she sent to my mom revealing the exciting news. "I was going to be a dog owner." I was overjoyed with the eager anticipation of my dream of being a dog owner beginning to take form, and so it was then that Hebat came into existence for me. Though I did not physically own him through his puppydom, I was the owner of Hebat since he was a pup. He used to be really red (in pictures), but now he has a luxurious golden coat. I made a video of myself, so I could let him meet me while he was still so young. This, of course, is so he would know who I was come time to meet me. And all be damn, it was love at first sight. We galloped to each other, and I dropped to all fours and hugged him while he profusely licked my face. He knew that it was me that was what sue had been training him for the past six months. During that time, he went with her on busses, to grocery stores, shopping malls, and doctor appointments. She got him used to be around people so that he would be used to being around them so he could attend UH Hilo with me. So, he was the UH mascot, and everyone knew and loved him. He made me more popular, but a lot of the time it was just him the people wanted to say hi to. You are not supposed to let people interact with a working service dog, but for me it was different. I saw that it was an important service for him to make me friends. People gathered around me a lot more often when I got Hebat and I would gladly share him.

The exercise was more fun with Hebat! We would go for "walk outs" where I would take him for a walk and bust out a workout on our way. We have stations along the way that I work out at when we are walking through campus, and I do yoga moves on the flat ground and practice inversions against school walls. Often, last summer I took Hebat to the Waikeloa duck ponds to swim. It was a perfect connection with nature experience for him, as I would kick a soccer ball or throw a stick into the water and he would eagerly swim out and retrieve it, all dripping with pond water and snorting. We had different locations around the pond that we visited. He frightened the ducks and Nene geese but could never catch them because they were too quick in the water and could fly on land.

Hebat has been a large focus of my life, as his responsibility prepares me for one day being a father. That is my dream to one day be a family man and Hebat helps teach me about the responsibility of caring for another being. When I become a father, I will be much more ready to take on the responsibility of being a dad from having endured my rat lung experience. Having Hebat has increased the joy in my life tenfold, even if I must work extra to keep him content; keeping a small human content will take far greater sacrifice on my part.

Lio, Hebat and I

30

"Spirit ball."

Spirit ball

A spiritual activity that I once played is a game my friend, Albert and I played with Hebat. It was a ball game we all played together. Albert and I tried to keep the ball away from Hebat, and Hebat tried to get the ball from us. Whenever he did get it, Hebat started snorting like a pig and didn't want to give us the ball, and so we had to chase him. It was exciting and fun, and the game seemed to continually evolve with Hebat. Time just seemed to fall away, and we got lost in the experience of trying to get the ball from each other. Quickly, ten minutes turned into an hour or even two. It felt like a spiritual experience, not just for me but for all of us. Every day, for more than a year, towards the end of the day, I would take Hebat out to the field behind my house to play soccer. But ever since Albert began to join Hebat and I, the game got way more fun. Possibly it was the addition of another human soul that was needed to elevate the game's enjoyment level high enough to make the experience become spiritual. That's how the games name developed "Spirit ball." When Hebat took the ball from one of us and started snorting like a pig, both Albert and I would start falling apart with laughter and then we taunt Hebat to give it back. This game of "spirit ball" connected the three of us in spirit. We were all hypnotized by the desire and effort to get the ball, and Hebat's consciousness was as tangled in the game as ours was. We had loads of fun together. I grabbed the ball from Hebat's rowdy snout, twisted and pulled it real hard, freeing the ball. I held it with my right hand and drop kicked it to Albert who was standing on the other side of the parking lot, waiting eagerly for the ball to come his way. Without a moment's hesitation, Albert fired the ball back with his strong leg. I got it and dribble it in front of Hebat, teasing him. Then I kicked it to Albert where he stood in front of the ball with his back to Hebat and did a stutter-step, teasing Hebat as well. Us teasing Hebat made him more fired up and engaged in the game. Hebat rushed Albert and snaked the ball again. The game would go on and on in circles with no particular outcome.

The fact that we all competed for the ball, but it was just a game, we were only playing, and there were no winners and losers, made it purely a spiritual practice which we did only for the pure joy of it. By the end, I was sweating bullets, and we were all winded. Hebat gets the ball and collapses to the ground for a laydown, panting real hard. Like any exercise game, we feel good with endorphins afterward. For us to continue this kind of play is beneficial for our spirituality; it keeps our bodies young as well as our spirits. Play and exercise are truly necessary to feed the spirit, increase happiness and give a person a wonderful sense of well-being.

31

"Grizzly Graham's Great Garden"

weedygarden

Recycled road pieces

The most recent garden I made was "Grizzly Graham's Great Garden." It was my pride and joy of accomplishments, besides myself of course. My book is right up there with them! This garden is in our current house of 221 B West Lanikaula. Once the land made up of "bunchy top banana trees and weeds" was ready for me to clear and start a garden, that's what I did! First, I built a table out of used pallets to foster my keki (baby) plants, which I had many of. A neighbor friend, Crystal Yamamoto helped me move the table just before she left for St Kitts for vet school, and my other friend Albert Talaroc-the same Albert that Hebat and I played "spirit-ball" with, helped me sand it and paint it bright green and yellow. When the table was finished, I dug away several inches of topsoil making a flat, egg-shaped surface of the land to put my nursery table upon. After the table was up, with the soil I harvested from the area for the table, I used the dirt to mix with potting soil from Home Depot. I also added rock dust and other soil amendments to make a rich garden bed for growing what turned out to be tomatoes of all sizes for the first crop. I made one more deep bed with big rocks to hold back the soil and grows a pineapple, kale, basil, spinach and a squash plant. We ate a lot of pasta sauce that summer, and veggies. Then I planted three little papaya trees about two feet tall each. Now they are all lengthy and fruiting eight foot+. That summer I also had planted nine baby papaya trees along the driveway, which are also bearing fruits now. Right now, my papaya surplus is copious! I sell them to the Locavore store, which sells all local cama 'Aina (from the land) food and my friends Cat and Arthur own and run it. Arthur has done much help in the publishing of my book-love, you man! In my garden, I planted a mango tree, which has deep dark green new growth of leaves right now. Giving it worm casting tea was responsible for this rich green color. I continued clearing back until I could reach as far as I thought I could go in my newly formed garden. I planted a good sized avocado tree that I got from a worm bin and I had grown in a pot, which was eventually transplanted into my biggest gardening pot, which is huge. I planted the tree in what I thought was going to be the end of my garden far to the back, but after my good buddy Harrison came and cut down the large Cecropin weed trees that were robbing sunlight from "my plants" and taking up valuable expansion room, there was so much more garden space for me to continue my endeavors. After he took out those trash trees I concentrated on multiple tasks at a time, often taking Hebat to the beach while I collected cloth bags and five-gallon buckets of beach media in the form of smooth pebbles, sand of different coarseness's and small driftwood pieces to cover my temple grounds, which is at the very top of the garden, overlooking my creation. I must give recognition to my mother, who would be our driver-love you mom! It was like garden exchange for free at Bayfront beach and Kings landing beach park, all I had to do was thank the ocean for supplying me with what I needed to make my garden beautiful.

My garden wore my energy out for the last time at the completion of my stone Ahu (altar) which I built in the back of my garden. It was a cool and misty/rainy day outside so the conditions were perfect for me hauling large rocks up to my Ahu site with a dolly, so that's what I did! The weather was good, but at one point I started to get exhausted and I felt like I should stop for the day. I would have too, but the weathers conditions were just so damn perfect, and so I listened to my mind, which told me to keep going. In not listening to my higher self, or intuition I choose against my own God will, which made me pay greatly. If you listen to your body and don't over-exceed its capabilities by listening to forced mind actions more enjoyable outcomes will be had. I continued searching out rocks that were part of a 1983 lava flow and pried them out with the leverage action of the 'O'o bar, which I was using. Just plunge the sharp end of the 'O'o bar into a crevice and heev. With leverage, a rock is often freed from your efforts. The very strong, stainless steel 'O'o bar that I was using was bent from my argues overwork of that session. For two days in a row I felt so terrible, miserable and depressed, but the effects of my plateauing were felt for much longer than two days. This was kind of routine for me to over expend my energy after ratlung, as my energy has been limited ever since its' damage was done on me. I have not worked out there but a very little bit since. I figure that having my energy is much more important than having a nice garden. In fact, I learned what a blessing it is to have energy at all! I had over-exceeded my body energy, which made me pay greatly! Even though it has never received much recognition as visitors seldom stop by, it is still the Greatest garden I have ever built. The important thing is that it gave my life a purpose and it connected me to mother nature and just was a way to occupy my time productively. The name of this garden is "Grizzly Graham's Great Garden" and is gave my life purpose and meaning during the summer of 2016.

32

"Ahu"

An Ahu is a traditional Hawaiian style shrine for making offerings. Mine, I dedicated to the spirit of Lanikaula, who is a God-like ancient Hawaiian warrior and the name of the street we live on. His spirit I welcomed to reside in my Ahu with offerings I made to . This empowers my temple far greater. Essentially an Ahu is a stack of stones or lava rocks piled in a square formation. The area of land that the Ahu is in is the grounds of the temple, which I cleared the weed vines that were growing in it and replaced them with drift wood chips from the beach. I brought countless five-gallon buckets of smooth beach pebbles and other beach media that I used for my garden. I collected these during trips that my mom and I would take Hebat to the beach with her Voltswanon gulf. I poured smooth beach pebbles around the Ahu structure, accentuating it further. I stacked rocks tightly together in a square shape, then poured some smooth rocks on the top, making it a flat surface to make my altar for God, where I put a buddha figurine, a bowl for holy water and an incense holder. There are also crystals and nice pieces of driftwood as decorations to adorn God's house. I also put a piece of drift wood that spells "Light up the Darkness-Bob Marley," which was gifted to me by Madison as a parting gift when her semester ended, and she went home last summer.

I make offerings regularly at my new Ahu, always giving appreciation for my already existent blessings and asking for guidance and blessings a new. I also make offerings to get Donald Trump out of office, as his ways of leading our country are convoluted. Each time I give a food offering, holy water, which I pour into a sacred bowl, a little "holy smoke" is offered and an incents must be lit to carry the essence of my prayers to the Gods in heaven. This is a physical, symbolic act of giving up possessions of value to me, which appeases God when you exude unattachment while in this physical body, for this world is after all temporal. Then there is the flower, which you must offer the essence of with your communication with divine entity. I use three flowers to offer in a prayer session because it seems like a good number, and not too greedy either. I pick my flowers at the "pua melemele" (yellow flower) bush, also called Allamanda. Last, I use an incense to send the essence of the flowers to divine realms (heaven) which is the source of all creation. To make prayers, pinch the flower so that you are holding it in front of your face vertically while pressing your palms together in prayer position. The butt of the flower should be pressed tightly together with the two middle fingers, while in prayer position. Your thumbs butt directly to your temple, between your eyes.

33

Offerings continued...

In Bali, I learned how to pray; I follow the same method they do to this day with slight alterations. There are several items you need to make effective offerings. First, you need an alter to make your offerings on, which is a structure elevated off the ground because anything being offered to the high God's must be kept elevated off the floor "like my Ahu." This is because the ground is where the Balinese believe the low gods inhabit. This is the Balinese belief, but my personal belief is slightly altered, however, as I sometimes drop a flower to the ground by accident when making offerings. I just quickly pick it up and hold it up above my head to the sky making an energetic zapping sound, and my belief is that by doing this it cleanses the flower, making it alright for offering to the high God's. I mean, I'm not going to go all the way to the kumu la'au pua mele mele-'yellow flower tree' to get another flower just because a flower fell to the ground while I was up at my Ahu making offerings; it's an energy thing, plus I am in Hawaii not Bali. I would never do this in Bali as the Balinese collective belief of the low gods staking claims to the ground is so strong that it would overpower my idea of holding the flower to the divine sky to purify the tainted flower. This is my personal belief and what you believe in becomes True because it is your personal belief, and what you believe is real! So, this works in my garden temples Ahu where my personal belief can be the dominating one. My belief about the left-hand right-hand taboo thing is not parallel to the Balinese either, as I wipe my butt with my right hand because that's what I am conditioned (used to) doing. The next thing you need to perform offerings like the Balinese is a food offering, as food is what sustains life and so must be appreciated. A bowl of holy water should be placed in front of a deity figurine for you to place the three flowers you must also obtain, in which you will use with an incense to send the essence of each flower with your prayers to God. One flower equates to one prayer, so you get three prayers per offering session.

34

At new location

Our new location is also right across the road to the UH, where my mom eventually started classes at and now has finished. It is a quarter mile from HCC Hawaii Community College, where I attended school. I went to the community college for four years before I transferred early to UH Hilo's Kinesiology and exercise science program. These years were spent mostly while living at my 331 B East Lanikaula residents. The only neighbors when we moved to our next place were a son and his mom, Teri and Hoku, who did not make much ruckus. The important thing is we were off that noisy road where we last had stayed so near to. We had moved to an oasis in the middle of Hilo that was right next to the school, which we needed it to be so that we could be students. My mom graduated last year with a master in conservation biology, and her final paper was on ratlung research, which is now her profession. Our new location is more conducive to being a student than our first Hilo house. Instead of hearing traffic out my windows I got to hear birds chirping, and the coqui frog is even present in my new location when the sun begins to set.

35

Additional Injuries to Ratlung

In addition to getting the opportunity to learn about healing through ratlung, I also sustained and recovered from two broken bones during my recovery time. My right scapula 7-15 then the left clavicle 5-16. Plus, just recently 7-29-17 I injured what I infer to be my meniscus. “A pulled Meniscus!” My inference is based off the research that I did on the internet which said that the affected part of my knee, which was the anterior region, is called the Meniscus. For all these types of injuries, restriction of movement is needed for recovery to occur. Any type of injury is the same in that with time and rest healing comes without conscious effort. Conscious effort can however increase recovery speed.

36

July 2015

"scapula"

My scapula break happened in Kauai when I raced a nine-year-old little girl on a cement basketball court and fell. Before that, I was chatting it up with the little girl and her mom earning respect and acceptance from the mother. I wanted to interact with her daughter as well, so I thought it would be fun to challenge the daughter to a foot race. We both agreed that the grass was too lumpy, so we agreed it might be dangerous to race on, so we decided to use the basketball court, which I tell you is unforgiving. Her mom did the countdown. "Racers ready on your marks, get set, go!" Like a couple of bolts of lightning, we shot across the court, but I was going too fast for my legs too keep up with. Rather than knowing my limits and respecting my boundaries, because I knew that my leg strength was much greater than this little girl was, I unleashed it. I was going to give it all I got! I wasn't accustomed to foot races yet though as I have never done one since ratlung. In listening to my mind and not my body (at that point I still wasn't able to decipher my mind from my True self "which is my body") my legs, which were moving like flash Gordon's, tangled up underneath me. I knew I was going down, so I thought I would roll to my back because I thought that would be the best bail out a method to not hurt myself. Nope though. "Aaaahhh" I shrieked in a high-volume low toned tone voice. The mom helped me up promptly, but the pain was so severe I knew something was broken. I freely cried tears of pain and sorrow for my beautiful body, as I sat with the sweet young mother and daughter and we figured the best place to buy ice from would be.

37

May-2016
"Clavicle"

My mind chatter is what caused me to crash my bike and break my clavicle-collar bone, that and the sidewalk was new, so it was slippery, that and I was riding a cruiser bike which I was not accustomed to riding. I was riding it like my Giant that was just stolen. In fact, that's why I was riding it, because along with grand theft auto, Hawaii is notorious for grand theft bicycles. It was taken because I could not find anywhere safe to lock it to so I was forced to leave my bike chained to a road sign downtown, so I could get a ride with my friend David Hubbard, Hilo's famous painter, to a potluck for Jacob Medina and Rachel Medina's wedding potluck, that we were both attending in HPP.

38

July-2017

"Meniscus"

I have deduced my most recent injury, the one which I am now experiencing the recovery of, to be meniscal damage. I don't know for sure if it was a torn meniscus but when I fell against that pillar, it made a click sound that I could feel internally throughout my body, which was accompanied by tremendous pain. I had pushed up off a university wall with my legs, walking them up to do a handstand. I noticed the pillars behind me, but I thought my inverted balance was good enough for them not to be impediments, which may cause injury. I went up and was up for two seconds, "but that's it," then I fell into the pillar, which cranked my leg lateral to my knee joint, making a click! My left leg was in pain that day, but by the next day, I knew it was an authentic injury.

39

Molokai healer woman

Last summer was a very pivotal point in my ratlung recovery when I was invited on a week vacation with a family of friends from my childhood, the Biddle family. They are from my hometown of Goodland Florida. They are the same family my mom, and I stayed with when we visited Goodland on our trip all the way to the Bahamas, but first, we went to Florida. Marian and Jamie were not present during that early trip. Nor were Ray and Amy much around, so it was magical to see all of them at once in Kauai. Though it was so much fun being with a group of mostly young people that was not my mom, it was also very difficult. Normal people (without TBI) operate at such a higher speed than I do! Trying to keep up with all the conversations and "just be like them" (which I am not) I am me, "a post ratlung survivor", was taxing on my energy and I started to get depressed but kept it inward. I was afraid to express my True feelings, so I didn't. Ray and Amy rented a beach house a mile up the hill from the beach, where we stayed. Being in a household of people unfamiliar to my condition was sort of unsettling because I felt ashamed that I had all these special needs. Why can't I just be normal, I thought! I knew that it was because of the life changing event that happened seven years prior to that point though. I was waking up much earlier than the rest of the crew, as I am so conditioned to do. Not getting good sleep made me get more emotional, as I do. My own fear of showing weakness while in a social group won, and so I didn't cry, I was just quiet. Molokai is quieter and much smaller than Big island, with one road wrapping around the island. On the fourth day, we went on a dive boat called Manu 'ele'ele or black bird, which was a-ways down the coast. Ray stayed home and watched the baseball game for this one. The nine-Mets are his favorite squadron! Our dive boat, "Manu 'Ele'ele," had a long tube that emitted compressed air, so you can take the tube down to the oceans floor, (about 15-20 feet) and breathe from it. There was a BC or buoyance compressor at the end to breathe from. I was blown away by how dead the reef was, all sun-bleached and dead. In comparison to the Bahamas pristine reefs that I experienced so frequently in the past, this was devastating. I was obviously witnessing the effects of climate change. After I swam, I laid on the wide black bow, perfect for heating up in the sun. All the exposure to the sun and being out on that boat tired me out and I got emotionally weak. I was so tired from the insomnia caused by the ratlung, which added up over the days. I did not hold back any more, I let everybody see my sorrow and exploded with tears. Everybody acknowledged my pain and accepted me more for being real with myself and everyone else. From there we all jumped in the car and went for pizza, then we went shopping for souvenirs. Ross and I drove back to the house to get my pipe and some smoke-medicine that I had failed to bring, then we met them at the pizza place. At the souvenir shop, there was an old lady who was the store keepers mother, and she was sitting in a metal office chair. She was observant that I was limping on my left side; my left knee flares up from an old wrestling injury when I am tired or under-rested ever since rat lung. It is like all my old injuries are irritated if I do not get proper rest. The lady looked wise. She was a Hawaiian kupuna (elder) with much knowledge of her ancestors and the art of healing. I know this because Amy and Ray bought me her book and it tells of her genealogy and her heritage. Hawaiians are very family oriented. She was bearded; long, black whiskers protruded from her chin. She said it holds her mana (power.) She is a healer! So, she offered to do healing on my knee. I was obliged to have her work on helping me feel better. First, she started belching and making swooshing sounds, while brushing the air around my effected knee behind her with her hand. I have had a number of healers work on me in Bali, and even in Hawaii, so I was familiar with the burping procedure as a means of clearing or moving stuck energy; a sign of a True healer! In fact, I do it (intuitively) when doing energy work on myself! Then she told me “each human child is born with a bowl of perfect light at their chest center and if he/she tends to that bowl it will grow in strength and one day the child can fly with the birds and swim with the sharks and do and know all things, hence be intuitive. I found this to be True. If we are fully connected with the present moment, we are just able to function more efficiently than if we are thinking about other stuff at the present moment. It is the present when we can be receptive with divinity, which is on this plane in the nature, especially during mornings and evenings, and expecially if you live in a hot-humid environment.

After Molokai is when I came back into myself and began to redevelop my God-given intuition. I had so many fears, which I mistook them for what life was. After my trip to Molokai last summer where I met the healer, and she reconnected me with myself, I had gone for a walk with Hebat through campus. This walk was not like walks before my trip to Molokai. I had all new presents in life and practiced at exercising my newly found intuitive self. I decided to connect with people and share some of the new Truth I had just received. I talked to the two girls sitting at the picnic table under cover at the campus center, and they were absorbed with what I said about sanctity to them. I told them that we (people) are natural divine beings and this plain that we live on (earth) is also a natural divine plain. Since we are both natural and from the same source, which is God, with God, we can also communicate and make direct manipulations in our own lives. I told them that we are amazing beings, and if we are connected to and in harmony with the present moment, we will also discover that we can receive human intuition through presents, where we can do and know anything. All that we have is the present moment, and that is the only place that God can be accessed, or noticed or recognized. Through present recognition and appreciation of life, you can access your own human amazement and life's amazements. I went home to take a nap, for all the oncoming Truth that I was channeling made me tired. As I laid down in my bed and started to drift off, something uniquely surprising happened to me. I experienced a translucent image of myself descend from above me and sink into my body. I felt more complete and whole after the remarkable experience. Later, shortly after that, I asked my mom to toss me the lighter when I was standing at the top of the three deep steps leading to our kitchen. Normally, I didn't catch things; they just bounced off my hands. It goes hand in hand with temporarily losing my intuition, I think a part of brain damage anyways. When she tossed that lighter to me, with ease, I caught it.

40

Truth

When you are connected to your True nature, you can do and know all things. In being connected, you will be intuitive, for you will feel your connection to God at all times. If you listen to your self and ask the creator for guidance, you will not get lost. I had experienced all of this during what I called "Truth week," when mud puddles appeared as realms to divinity. I still did not feel good, and it had been going on for a long time, so my ego mind was very activated. I know this because worries and fears would come quickly, noticeably depleting my energy. Instead of following orders from my mind like usual, I attempted to follow my spirit, and let that guide me on Hebat and my walk. That and I just let Hebat guide, even if I did not really feel like going that way. I would just allow whatever comes up to come up and sometimes even witnessing miner miracles. Whenever I allowed myself to snap into presence, my energy was high, and the words that the healer in Molokai had told me rang strong through my head. "If you are connected to your True nature you can swim with the sharks, and fly with the birds and do and know all things." We already know this because it is innate inside us! We just must trust and be brave. This knowing, if you make it a new belief, will become your new reality. This awareness is how you reach God in the present moment, for you will be present enough to see the signs along your path. When you are present and in harmony with your True nature you will have super strength, and can easily accomplish tasks that you set your mind to. It is just like that, we conceive an idea in our head, then if we work to pursue that tasks completion, and we will witness the manifestation of the object of your mind's desire. From mind, to action, to manifestation into real form. "It's magic!" Or, is it just regular? We are magicians, but we are not conscious of this, therefore our powers remain undiscovered. Our unique human capabilities are not recognized as unique because we all have human potential abilities. We then look at our unique capability as mundane and ordinary, even boring. Then we get depressed with the seeming smallness of our lives. Life feels empty and meaningless when we are just living for instant gratification of modern technology like is so often the case in this modern world. All that we really need to live a happy meaningful life is to be present and abide by our natural law, which is "we are nature." We must act in accordance with our feminine nature! We need to have both feminine and masculine, but the female is closer to God at nature, so we can't be unbalanced with an overabundance of masculinity. The world has been patriotically run for the past sixteen hundred years and we have encountered numerous wars and acts of unjustness between fellow human beings. These acts of unjustness were brought into play with the egoic masculine mind, which creates separation and superiority of one race. We must be receptive to each others frequency, making regular exchanges of Love. The qualities of unconditional love, compassion, wisdom, beauty, gentleness, patience, acceptance, forgiveness, nurturing, welcoming, accessibility, kindness, intuitive, and healing are all present in divine feminine nature. We must not make unjust acts that are out of harmony with nature; this includes greedy selfishness and the unwillingness to share with others, for this disconnect is the unobserved mind, who acts from a place of fear, where greed and disconnected selfishness, ego reside. So, it is an imposter to what is True, and it may try to deceive you with sparkly material glamor or other false promises. Through appreciation and present receptibility to your own God nature you will prosper with your life's endeavors.

41

Healing

Because we are organic beings from the earth, we have a miraculous healing ability. A sick-wounded human being can be compared to a sick-wounded plant because we are both natural beings and healing happens innately similar for both of us. Healing just happens! If given the medicines to promote accelerated and complete healing, the healing process will be enhanced and occur more quickly. "Let food be thy medicine!" Whatever you put into your body matters and it will have an effect, positively or negatively on your being. This is certain when it comes to healing from moderate breakdown of a long, arduous hike, but diet is most crucial in recovery from serious injury.

42

Human conditioning

Do you know yourself truly, or do you falsely identify with the talker in the head, the false sense of self, or the ego? Who do you let be in charged? Likely the answer is both. Fear and deep pain bring out the ego, this can be both emotional and physical pain. That is why someone who is hurt emotionally or physically may be reactional because that is the nature of the ego and they may be inflicted with ego. We (who are conscious) should not be reactional ourselves and get mad at those people who are not aware of how they act, rather we just need to have compassion for those individuals. Have compassion that they see not clear, but rather are trapped behind a cloud of delusion. If you react to how they are being, or rather "being controlled by their minds," then your reaction will allow your ego to operate, which strengthens it and the madness will perpetuate. Egos activate other egos when present, and if the perceiving mind is not strong and present enough to recognize it as ego, then they will be deceived and be reactional as well. If you are not conscious enough of a being, then your ego will become activated.

. When you are controlled by the ego, you are unaware that this is happening, and you make choices that are out of harmony with nature and do not make sense, like America's president Donald Trump. He is as much controlled by his ego as Adolf Hitler was during the Holocaust. We must heal before we are able to live. That is, we must first erase our accumulated human conditioning before we can truly live. Until you can see the conditioning and then, make a conscious choice not to be it just because that's how our collective perception of life is "so you must act in a certain way." Example: go to church because others do, and you are a sinner if you don't.

Only when you can recognize human conditioning for what it is can you begin to break it. Human conditioning is a "belief" or 'dream' that life is the way that it has been told to you as if other people know what life is about. All types of conditioning in life are built with repetition. It is the ego or "false self" who just goes along with what other people say and do that is a conditioned human. This is not expressing True nature! It is the unconscious self who is mind controlled by the dream of the planet, and it is the conditioned mind that is filled with fear. It is not the True Self. Only you (us) can know what we want and have the will-power/choice-power to accomplish it. When you can recognize your True God thoughts as so and choose to act them out rather than the other thoughts that are fear/worry based, even if the God thoughts don't seem to make sense to your logical mind, this is where you will find salvation. That is the egoic mind that tries to scare us from our Truth. This is another reason why it is so important to be receptively present because then you can have enough presents to recognize the thoughts that emerge in your mind and Truly be able to decipher True God-thoughts from False-ego (deceiver) thoughts. So, it is our work in life (peoples) to recondition ourselves to have enough present receptivity to see the divinity that is on this earth, which is in every animal and human being and natural object (tree, plant, stone.) Present meditation is required for this. It is easier for some people to break the conditioning pattern than others due to their upbringings may be conducive to be less conditioned, i.e., they did not watch television at childhood, spent a lot of time outdoors ext.. Therefore they are less conditioned than others who watch tv and are always indoors playing video games throughout life. This type of behavior subliminally brainwashes people, distorting their behavior and making them unaware and become taken over by their own mind. The longer you have lived in the conditioned state without a glimpse out and believed it to be a reality, the harder it will be to break the conditioning and experience life for what it really is, which is boundless amazement! The stronger you believe/perceive the falsity to be a reality, the harder it is if not impossible to deprogram. The nature of the human being is to start absorbing and learning immediately after birth. We are like absorbent sponges and information, or our outside surroundings (including people) is the liquid that is absorbed. If we continue to perpetuate the dream of the planet to remain as is, i.e., remain unconscious, then we may be doomed as a species.

Human evolution is but a choice. It is a conscious choice. It's a choice to be conscious. Human evolution is a bunch of choices, all of them being in harmony with our truth, which is consciousness and love, not unawareness and fear. To be open and allowing for life to flow through you is a choice of love, whereas being closed-off to yourself, others and the diversities of life is a choice of fear. This is because life is diverse, so we must be comfortable with accepting and allowing those diversities to exist. We need to accept diversities because we ourselves are diverse beings and self-acceptance is crucial. Being evolved is making conscious, considerate, compassionate choices all the time; make it be like a first nature because that is how we are intended to be in our True nature. This is divine feminine nature; mother nature. Unkindness stems from fear or ego, i.e., not being aware. Human connection rather than human division is what I'm talking about. We are moving into the age of Aquarius, moving out of 6,500 years of patriarchal madness and into our True divine feminine selves. We must be aware that this is what is going on at a planetary level so we too can jump on board the wagon and evolve. Evolution is a choice this time! If you do not allow the evolution to occur through acceptance and allowance, then you will be left behind in the madness of the current Trump reality, following the belief of the planet, which is flawed and convoluted. So, this time evolution is a choice, and we must make it to avoid extinction! When we are conscious or present is when we are tapped into our True divine feminine human nature. The qualities present in the sacred feminine-True human nature are compassion, unconditional love, beauty, wisdom, gentleness, patience, acceptance, forgiveness, welcoming, accessibility, kindness, and healing. All those traits you will receive when you allow yourself the connection. When you are connected to your True nature, not being swayed by fears and worries of the mind you can do all and know all things. You will have keen intuition like a built-in GPS, allowing you to make correct choices that benefit the self, as well as the whole. Your energy becomes fully connected to the here and now, which is always what is, and from this, you will not be misdirected in your path by following someone else's.

43

Getting better

Ratlung slowed me down to the world. That is, I was slowed down, and the world continued to go at the same pace. This allowed me to witness the changes that were occurring outside of me with time, which is speeding up now. That is how a Monday will become a Friday quite suddenly. Or is it that technology is speeding up our brain's perception of time? Evidence has found that our constant use of technology is making our brains more effective and efficient at processing information. This results in tricking us into thinking time is going faster than it is. (National geographic)

I look like a normal guy now; well damn near. I still have a lot more recovering to go. My double vision throws me off time to time. Most of the pain that I still have is an emotional pain I get from being so tired, which has been reoccurring recently, and from being so secluded, which brings me down, and now is a constant. Everything gets confusing when I am tired and is more difficult to deal with. My mind automatically reminds me of what I don't have, but I want so much of the time (a divine feminine lover.) Before ratlung I didn't experience these sorts of dilemmas as severely. The contrast of my life experience now from before I was so sick is vast. It is like my human condition was exacerbated with ratlungs sickness. I used to have a life where I interacted with people regularly, where I had friends, and I laughed. I have not experienced this severity of depression before. I am grateful for my blessings in life, but a positive change must occur in my life in order for me to feel fulfillment and feel alive again. I must pull myself up and just know that my situation is about to change and this hell that I am experiencing will not last forever. I am about to move to Newport Beach CA, which will bring me a social life like I have not imagined and girls galore. Finally, I will reach fulfillment in all areas of my life-physical-relationships-social and spiritual to bring me happiness. Never again will I doubt myself or self-criticize. Anything is possible!

I often look back and remember where I came from. It is amazing that the mangled mess that was me transformed into the shapely being I am today. With the daily consistency of a good lifestyle, if given the proper ingredients, an injured body can thrive again. I have seen it numerous times with baby trees, which are organic beings of the earth like us. I have a tree nursery of all the volunteers that sprout up in my worm bins. I am a worm farmer by trade, "Graham the Worm-man." With the castings from the worms (worm poop,) which is a proper life-sustaining ingredient for plants, I am able to resurrect a near dead baby tree. Just apply castings and water with additional worm casting tea, put in a place with good sun, keep watered and wait. Worm castings are chocked full of beneficial microorganisms that benefit plants greatly. It might be a couple days, but plants will respond almost instantaneously by germinating bright green new growth foliage. It will work for an older growth tree as well. I did the same thing for a nearly dead orange tree that grows in my yard. The tree that has not fruited in years now boasts fruit today as long as I continue to give it the life-sustaining elixir, "worm casting tea." I learned with my own case that it works the same for humans. Not with ingesting worm casting tea but with the right ingredients/superfoods such as Spirulina, Chlorella and a number of Chinese herbs in addition to good nutrition and an active lifestyle. Because plants and animals are both of the earth, hence natural or made by God, they both have innate healing powers if given the proper healing life-sustaining earthly ingredients.

It is possible to bring a seemingly incurable person "according to the Western medical system beliefs" to a state of harmony if the proper life-sustaining ingredients are met in a timely manner. For best results, early treatment should be applied. The plant kingdom is different than the animal kingdom in that plants are quite stationary to one place, whereas animals require movement. Only a body in motion is a body that can be pain-free. For plants, you can just apply the right ingredients, such as nourishment through microorganisms and adequate sunlight, and then the plant will one day regain its natural state. However, with a human being, it is a little different. Humans need daily movement in order not to deteriorate or seize up. That is why in the hospital I was so lucky to have my mom, who gave me daily massage and range of motion. That is a large reason why when I came out of the coma I was able to regain movement as quickly as I did. Inactivity promotes decay and discomfort whereas an active lifestyle encourages healthy growth and equanimity. Combining good nutrition and healthy movement in the form of physical exercise is key when it comes to reaching this state of balance when recovering from a serious injury. Nutrition is number one, for the quality of energy that you put into your body is the kind of energy that you will produce with your body. So, diet comes before exercise because the body must consume calories to operate and if the quality of the food you consume is poor and low, then that will be your energy output, "poor and low." Take your pick, would you want to put dead foods, void of vital energy into your body as the source of fuel, or superfoods, which live up to their name? I know that my human organism responds better to whole real foods than fake processed foods, so that is what I choose to consume.

44

5-21-17 Churchy me

This morning while walking Hebat through UH campus I could hear a beautiful south pacific islander sounding song coming from a choir. Hebat was sniffing some bush and in so disallowing me to go hear them sing. I said "shishi" and then he peed on the bush and we headed on our way, which passed just above the choir on the walkway. I shouted, "Hana ho" meaning "again (actually 'more work)" in Hawaiian. I asked if they were a Samoan choir? One of them answered me "it's for anyone, black, white all colors are welcome." Then a female member said service is at ten in UCB 100; you should come! Usually, I wouldn't have went, but I could see it as an opportunity from God to get an inside look at how a church operates. UCB 100 was my old classroom for I had many classes in the past there, so I knew exactly where it was. I asked what time it was, and they replied nine thirty. I thanked them and headed on my way. Usually, I would never enter a church; the idea of sitting through a sermon is just too brain washing and convoluted for me. Every opportunity that arises in life is God sent and created by divinity. It is also created with your own mind and True desires. We can consciously work with divinity to direct or richen our lives, which is done through self-awareness. This is an important reason for staying positive and being aware of your thoughts. It is important to learn not to pass opportunities up "because they are created by divinity and your own mind, and may yield beneficial fruits for you. This is also why it is important to be consciously aware of your and everybody's amazement because it will be everyone's belief, there hence "be an amazing reality."

So, I went and watched the service after I returned from my workout with Hebat. I was nice and sweaty to go sit in UCH 100's air-conditioned room and cool off. Several speakers went up, and the first one told us of hardship that happened in her life, which brought her humility. She experienced suffering during her childhood for her parents were unjust. Then she found God through Christ, "which saved her." The others spoke of miracles occurring through Jesus as well. Everything that speakers were saying was concise with the Truths that I have been learning through my prayer to the full moon, except credit for the miracles in the guest speaker's stories would automatically be credited to Jesus, as if miracles can only occur through Jesus Christ. Though they talked about miracles and overcame hardships that lead to humility and awakening, the Christian religion believes that miracles only occur through Jesus Christ, when we all share the same potential as Christ did and we can all be conduits to miracles happening through divinity, which involves us. I went to that sermon because I saw it as an opportunity to experience church without being too involved, and just sitting in the back row of UCB's air-conditioned room cooling off with Hebat. I was intrigued with the unexplained phenomena they spoke of, only they mistakenly believe that miracles occur through Jesus Christ alone. For this reason, the Christian religion discredits themselves as amazing wonders, for mistakenly believing Christ is to be the only conduit to miracles. At the end, they had a coir and great songs which lured me there in the first place!

45

Operating as a human

People must first learn how to operate their human vehicle before they can know their potential or how to use their magic human powers. The power of manifestation, or using the mind to create what it is you desire is one magic power that we possess. This power is so normal and average that we consider it the norm and then it becomes mundane, so we don't think a thing of it. In fact, all thoughts if concentrated and focused on will yield a physical manifestation of those thoughts. Animals are not able to create anything they want. Or perhaps it is that animals do not have the ability to conceive desires outside of their basic survival. Just having a desire alone will begin the process of creating your thought to become a reality. What humans have that animals do not have are opposable thumbs and forebrains. Therefore, humans have these abilities beyond animal's abilities. This is also why people have egos whereas animals do not. It is like a price that humans must pay to be human and possess all these creative capabilities and unique potential. We also must carry the ego's heavy burden, which is the human condition and can make us very unhappy. God granted man the ability to do and know all things under one condition, which is "the human condition" or ego. We have a false identity that becomes us if we are not aware of this fraud. We must distinguish our True selves from our ego. We are granted creative powers beyond any other species, but we have the difficulty of having two identities. One is the real you or "your Truth," and the other is the false you or "the ego." They are both inherent in each human being; they are the dualities of this life, "Truth and ego." It is our duties to see Truth as so and live it. The next time you find yourself in an argument with somebody, recognize if your ego is present. Were you reactional and driven by emotions? If so that was probably not you but your ego. You will know if it is "Truth or ego" if one or both of you get so upset that you begin to yell and defend your position, or even use physical violence. The ego is out of control emotional turmoil.

46

Declaration

It is my intention, "or goal" to see that the completion of this book comes before August 2017, when I begin my program that specializes in "ABI" acquired brain injury in Newport Beach California. Coastline Community college is one of five TBI schools that there are in the country. It is a one-year program that helps a person with ABI (me,) compensate for deficits acquired from brain injury. Though I feel like calling it quits sometimes, keep going I must. There is a bright light glowing in the distance for me, and it's Newport beach California

47

Current Situation

I have currently not been enjoying my life's experience. It's balls hot in Hilo, and I feel void of purpose. I feel forgotten about. It is like everybody forgot what I went through or it is that they don't know I have been through anything at all. That's how good of a job I did at recovering! Now I just look like a regular guy;

something that I was not expected by doctors to do from that mangled mess I was. I gotta give myself credit for that one, but no "my conditioned self-compares me to others and tells me I'm not good enough." That's how healed I am, whereas I used to not self-critic or compare my situation to others, bringing me down, stunting my healing. All that was important to me before I stopped out of school was that I eat good, exercise, make offerings and do my homework. My life had meaning. That was the focus of my life energy throughout the time I spent in school, was to recover inside and out. Homework was a recovery method in its own. My prior years of physical training paid off when I had chosen not to go to school on the second semester of last year. So, I had to focus strictly on house chores and attempting to make an income in the time since the school was. I have sold composting worms and worm bins and have made just several hundred bucks. "but gotta give appreciation for every dollar!" Making money in this world proves difficult without a college degree, that is why I plan to attend a one-year program on adapted brain injury at Newport Beach California. It is one out of the five TBI certificate programs in the country. This is to get me ready for the next step in life. Coastline is a stepping stone, helping someone with brain damage succeed. Next I will go to Massage school in Fullerton Community College, a two hour drive from Newport beach, so Hebat and I will have to get an apartment there and that is where I will step into real indipendants.

Every day is my duty to have the house looking nice for when my mom gets home from work. If it's clean she's happy, and things are alright but if the place is not to her likings she gets mad, and things are not so fun in my world. I am way better now, so keeping up with the cleaning, constantly cleaning up after myself is more manageable now than a couple of years back. Dishes are ever going, so long as I am continuously eating and producing dishes. Dishes often called for a medicinal bongy in order to complete the task. Washing dishes is an activity that I am sure anybody can benefit from a little smoke before undertaking, especially if they have any pre-resistance to doing it.

Repression is something I am now used to; as time passes and I am still without a female counterpart whom I feel starved for, and my age continues to increase. Living with my mom for so long has had its difficulties, especially as I become older and more healed. I feel so trapped sometimes, more so when I am healing from an injury so I must be sedentary," like now with my meniscus damage." The continuation of my life remaining as is without change for the better would be anti-progressive to my livelihood. So, I was extremely melancholy today.

The reason I want to write an informational transformational book is because of the desire I once had of becoming a healer. I am now taking the appropriate actions to write an inspirational book intended to offer healing to the dysfunctional human psyche with my life experiences and acquired life knowledge. I have gone back to school since ratlung, where I learned how to be an effective writer, so I can write this book of my story because it is my inner desire and so my Truth to follow. I am writing this book because I feel that it is my work to compile the useful information that I have learned in my life to share with others. I prayed for Truth not for just myself, but for all humans to learn from.

48

Why it is so critical to be in the present moment

God is active in the present moment. That is when miracles occur. The past is the past; it has already happened! The future is yet to happen, but your present choices and actions including thoughts and desires play a direct influence on the future, which becomes the present. This is why God can only flow through you in the here and now. “In the present moment, you can do and know all things, hence be intuitive.” That is to say, when you are tapped into or connected to the present moment and your “True self”, not lost in worries or fears of the mind or the conceptualized belief of who you are through your career, socioeconomic status ext., it is possible to have super strength and innate wisdom and supreme decision-making capabilities. I felt this directly during what I call “Truth week,” when colors were more vivid and mud puddle reflections more impressionable. Again, suffering brought out the awakening experience for me. The sufferings main source was my mind, which was engulfed with such fears and worries, and I took orders from it for a long time, disallowing my happiness to flow.

Whenever I let my actions come from a place of fear or unconsciousness, things do not go well, and I am not efficient with my time and resources. When I am present with what is than fear does not emerge. If we practice being present and not being controlled by the mind, our consciousness will become strengthened, and we will become better at being present, “or better at life!”. You can find purpose and meaning in simply being, ie. eating, sleeping, walking/hiking, pooping, doing the dishes and having sex. It is when you let yourself be swayed by "your troubles-worries, that you are not being present with life, which extends beyond worries. Worries and fears are part of the human condition, and we are but to understand them as not "Truths of life" and so choose not to express or live-out those fear-based actions.

I used to have an eating disorder at twenty years old, anorexia nervosa, which marks another time in my life when I was under control of my mind. This was just after my trip to India, where I saw all the Indian people for four and a half months, who are thin in the figure. There are many yogis in India, and that is what I was, an inspiring yogi. The food in India facilitates digestion and makes for a good poo, or should I say, "a poo not hard to push out." When I came back to America, I would compare the lifestyle differences of the US diet to back in India. American food did not facilitate digestion, which is often not even given any consideration. When I was back from India, I was enamored with eating Indian food at the nearby Indian restaurants in Berkeley. I would always ask for the Fennel at the end as it would aid my digestion and make for a nice poo.

49

Communication

Communication is one of man's greatest gifts. Misuse of communication is one of man's biggest curses. Where communications misuses real roots are from is unconsciousness or the ego. You can make somebody feel good by talking kind words to them. Likewise, you can feed people poison with your words by saying something hurtful, creating emotional pain inside the other. This is the actions of the ego! The ego is merely the reactional you that pretends to be you. The ego tricks us in this way. Humans are the only animals with a capability to yack like people do, aside from some flock birds maybe. This is people's ego who yacks senselessly because True nature would not have the need to fill space with such noise. Having been so slowed down to how I used to be, makes it difficult for me to join mindless-trivial conversations like I once could; it is because this is really energy extensive for me to do so.

It is possible to be connected to divine energy all the time. Being connected to True nature makes you feel as if you are high on LSD because you can attain a similar state of presents with LSD as being simply high on life. If you are so keenly present and have ever experimented with LSD before, you will understand this fact. So, with intense presence, it is possible to achieve the same state of presence as dropping acid. This does not consist of common mind chatter, but rather complete openness and receptivity to what is going on, to life. We must allow life to flow through us, attuning our wills to God's will. It helps to spend time out in nature often, but also sharing a human connection is vital in health and prosperity, "I can feel that one!" If you are attentive in your life and really listen to your Truth, and follow it, you will not drift astray from your True path, or from lasting fulfillment. When you follow the voice of the false identity by following selfishness, however, you may be burned each time.

50

DOH negligence

From my chair at our dining table, I have heard so many ill-spirited conversations my mom has with ratlung victims, whose lives have been devastated by this emerging tropical disease. As you age, ratlung has more debilitating, devastating effects and renders a person unable to care for themselves. This results in them needing a care giver or someone to help take care of them. My mom has been my "paid" (not much), caregiver. A ratlung victim named David came over to my house accompanied by his caregiver. I know like three other ratlung survivors named David, each whom I call "Ratlung Dave." This David had the disease for ten years and felt like ever since he moved back to Hawaii from where ever he was in the mainland, after having gotten it in Hawaii in the first place, that he was getting worse after he came back to Hawaii. "He said that he was going downhill." He was really depressed and in the midst of suffering. Like most ratlung victims who get it bad, and especially if they are alone and live in the jungle in Puna, which is a thirty-minute commute to any store or town, they don't recover. Negativity and low

Hawaii island Department of Health DOH is largely responsible for the widespread outbreak of ratlung worm in the Hawaiian-islands. They are responsible because of their negligence of knowing about ratlung, which has been in Hawaii for over ten years, and not alerting the public. They did not want to inform the public because of their fear of tourists finding out and then not wanting to come to Hawaii as their vacation destination anymore. In fact, DOH claim that ratlung is not a food born illness, when in fact it Truly is! A plain-simple example just to justify my point: Somebody eats some lettuce from their garden thereby contracting ratlung. Is too a food born illness! This is the same kind of preposterous insanity which Donald Trump exudes in his insane, ignorant acts. Instead, they made up lies that medical personals tell patients, which is "it will get better in two weeks." When it is two weeks-time that these parasites need in order to reach the brain, where the neurological part of the illness comes into play. The state of Hawaii plans to give out a million-dollar grant going to ratlung alleviation-work. My mom works at the College of Pharmacies with Dr. Susan Jarvy as a ratlung researcher. "She is basically a scientist without a Ph.D.!" They say it is not a totally done deal yet, but the governor plans to give the funding to DOH, when Dr. Susan Jarvy's group of ratlung researchers, which my mom is part of, really deserve it. This is the same kind of corruption that always seems to happen in the corporate world, involving the people appointed to be in Power. I am exposing these facts about the Hawaii Department of Health because this book is about Truth, therefor even the ugly must be exposed."

DOH acts in this way because they are not being True nature, which is of divine properties and of total interconnectedness. There are people who suffer in a great deal of pain and go unnoticed because people think it's not a big deal "you'll get better in two weeks 'NOT!'" Humans, like bee and ant colonies, are a collective species and all need to work together at one purpose. That means that we are all of one collective conscious-being, and in the system that we have set up to help protect the people, DOH is not doing their job. They are choosing (still) to not inform people because of their fear of tourists finding out.

51

6-14-2017 Mr. negativity

As time nears closer to August when I am to leave Hilo, I cannot help from feeling bitter and angry about things in my life, like the constant continuation of me always sitting at this kitchen chair that I have sat at to do my studies for the past long time, or failed relationships that turned into "them being an enemy toward me," or just boredom in this house in the heat of Hilo. Not to forget the sexual frustration that I have experienced. Now it's 7:30 so it is still cool out, but come ten o'clock, eleven for sure, the heat is too great to go outside without overheating. It was not like this previous summer's because I feel that global warming has reached an extreme high, which it has not yet gone to until this summer. Like water travels through a colander, I will let this experience pass through me-just that fast and easily!

My life experience has been exceedingly difficult lately. As Hawaii's summer continues to build in heat, making mornings before ten o'clock, and after four o'clock in the afternoon the only times to be outside without overheating. When I am driving in the passenger seat with mom in her old Volkswagen gulf, during the hours of between eleven and three o'clock, the impending heat of the day feels as if it is driving nails into my body! My second Giant bicycle was stolen two days ago, so that makes transportation so much harder for me. "Fucking thieves!" The temperature is only going to continue to build through my departure to Newport in August. My mom leaves for work at nine in the morning and comes home after five, so it is a long stretch until I can get a ride somewhere from her. I used to stay occupied with my garden while she is gone in the day, which would make me feel productive and occupied, but ever since I burnt my energy out in the construction of my Ahu several months ago, I have worked in there very seldom. I still make offerings to the divine mother, but my enthusiasm about it is less as my enthusiasm about my life has also been low. I have been in this same place at 221B West Lanikaula, underneath the University of Hilo for so long now and now I am not a student, so I do not feel like I have a purpose here, nor do I want to be here. Sadness visits me every day now, as I find myself crying in front of the bathroom mirror because being without a routine makes me confused. In addition to crying in front of the mirror, I also wander by it from time to time and sing a song or make an impersonation or do something to make myself smile. It used to make me smile, but after the eight hundredth time, it just became so routine that it lost its flavor and is no longer funny to me. This time now, eight and a half years after my parasitic infection, before I leave for my new life in Newport is most possibly the most difficult part of my ratlung recovery. This is because I am currently the most aware of my situation that I have been since ratlung did its insidious damage on me. I am now an intellect! This is due to my impending complete recovery and is because of my proactivity since day one. Increasing my "Brain food" supplementation intake under my acupuncturist, Dr. William Pettis's word is one leading factor that brought me back into a state of normality too.

52

Walk my talk

I have conquered depression numerous times in my life, and now with the faith that "I will be happy again one day," I will not let this depression take me over for the rest of Hilo's grueling hot summer that I am yet to endure. Instead, I will count my already existent blessings, which will magnify the bounty being manifested in my current life for giving appreciation for the blessings I have. As I use my time productively writing the particular things in this book, I feel lighter and as if I am letting go of negativity and depression as I write this. It is as if writing this book is cleansing me, or healing me. I just must be present at this moment here before I leave for Newport beach so I will develop a habit of present appreciation to bring with me there. Knowing that I am going to Newport beach soon helps to remind myself that I am not here in Hilo doing nothing forever, soon the physical factors of my world will change completely, also shaping and changing all of me. I must give thanks for this time that I have where nothing is going on, and I have no obligations, so I can write my book while the experience is still fresh in my mind, and it has not been erased by other experiences.

So, even though boredom, depression, and listlessness are frequent now, I will trust that I will experience their opposites again in this dualistic world. This time where I have no obligations (besides recovery-continuation) was given to me by the hands of God to complete my book. Though inspiration is not flowing through me like it once was, I am going to empty the dark stones that accumulated in my once brightly shining bowl of light so that I can shine bright again. And so, I say the ancient Hawaiian healing art of Ho'o'pono'pono unto myself, "I'm sorry, please forgive me, I love you, I forgive you." From this point on I will travel with a full bowl of light at my chest center, attracting bounty, prosperity, and abundance. That is solidified in the writing of this book!

53

A Closure

So, with asking my prayer for Truth to the full moon so long ago, I continued to hold trust that my prayer would be complete with the solidification of my full recovery. I prayed for Truth so that I could obtain humility and Truth of life. The fact that this sickness is based off a prayer, and that now I look like a normal person, when I used to look like Frankenstein, or that I survived and am now doing so well instead of died or remained in a state of dysfunction is proof enough for me that God exists and is communicable. I now feel ready to receive a lover and co-create an offspring or two with her when the time comes and then rear them together, making me the family man I so desire to be. First, I must sink into my happiness; I asked in my prayer to the full moon that I would end up a better person, to myself and to others, with more self-love and more love for others, and a full True happiness will overcome me.

-End-

ABOUT AUTHOR

Hi, my name is Graham. I am a very outgoing, rather meticulous person with a drive like no other. Perhaps that is what made me able to make it back to myself after being so changed by ratlung. "I never gave up!" I used to think of myself as a Truth seeker, but now I am a "Truth seer for I have been granted my Truth prayer."

My life now is so much different than ten years ago (before the coma.) Back then I was an active surfing/skateboarding guy. Now I am not able to be so active yet because of some circumstances. I am as active as possible though like going to the gym, doggy walk yoga, walking and/or running, going to the beach, surfing sometimes. I know that "a bodie in motion keeps on going."

I am a very nice guy. I love to flirt and interact with feminine beings (ladies.) I also like cool dudes who also carry traits of divine feminine energy (which is explained in the book.)

My prior travels in third world/developing countries awakened me to the amazement that life is enough so that I could see plainly that there was/is a dysfunction in the mental structure of most Americans (including Westerners.) That is one factor that made me ask a prayer for Truth to a full moon, so that I could one day teach about this false identity everybody has. They (Americans with Americanized conditioning) are just not as authentic, fun, joyous, kind, generous, sociable and all around loving as the nice foreign people in the distant reaches of the globe, like the ones who kindly invited me into their homes and always fed me something. This is due to the conditioning that humans inherit from where they develop throughout life (geographically where one lives.) Fear is what causes this phenomenon of unfriendliness in the West to exist. Fear is where the ego operates from! People become angry because of being afraid, which leads to feeling appended and then make assumptions (which there is no validity in.) In the West we are taught to fear through advertisements, news broadcasts(especially with a slant,) politicians ext. This is to keep the mass sheeple (people) in line and repressed. So, that is our reaction is to fear. We must see that fear is a delusion that holds us back from our dreams. If we mindlessly follow the masses because of fear then we will never discover our human potential. Heaven is on this plain (earth) and if our perception is right we will view ourselves as divine beings and will discover our unique human abilities.

Made in the USA
Columbia, SC
24 July 2021